# Marketing Alignment

*Breakthrough Strategies for Growth and Profitability*

The Path to Market Leadership

*by Mac McKinley*

**Marketing Alignment: Breakthrough Strategies for Growth and Profitability**

Copyright © 2002 Mac McKinley

All rights reserved. No part of this book may be reproduced or transmitted in any form or by any means without the written consent of the publisher.

Published by Hats Off Books™
610 East Delano Street, Suite 104
Tucson, Arizona 85705
ISBN: 1-58736-118-3
LCCN: 2002094423

# READ ME FIRST – *EXECUTIVE GUIDELINES FOR USING THIS BOOK*

*Marketing Alignment* is a practical guide that will help you optimize your sales and marketing efforts. The end result of proper sales and marketing alignment is increased market share and revenue, and reduced marketing costs (as a percentage of revenue). Read this book, incorporate the principles of sales and marketing alignment into your own business, and your company will again be on the path to market leadership.

If you are really time constrained and cannot read the entire text, here is a synopsis of the chapters with shortcuts a reader could take and still gain specific levels of knowledge on Sales and Marketing Alignment.

**Chapters One and Two**—read these chapters to understand the basics of Sales and Marketing Alignment.

**Chapters One, Two, Three, and Six**—read these chapters to gain a strong working knowledge of Sales and Marketing Alignment.

**Chapters Four and Five**—read these chapters to learn and fully comprehend the Sales and Marketing Alignment process. These chapters also include numerous examples of market-leading companies that use the principles of Sales and Marketing Alignment every day to maintain their competitive advantage.

Determine the specific level of knowledge on Sales and Marketing Alignment you would like to gain, then read the chapters that correspond with that objective.

Or, use the following guidelines:

**CEOs**—read Chapters One, Two, Three, and Six, or e-mail me at goalpath@att.net to set up a briefing on how Marketing Alignment can help your company.

**CFOs**—read Chapters One, Two, Three, and Six.

**Sales VPs**—read the entire text.

**Marketing VPs**—read the entire text.

**Aspiring Junior Executives**—read the entire text twice.

**Sales and Marketing Managers**—read entire text, then highlight Chapters Four and Five, and keep that text within easy reach on the top of your desk.

**Harvard and Ivy League MBAs**—this is practical rather than theoretical knowledge, so read it at your own risk.

**Texas Business School Graduates and MBAs**—grab a six-pack of Shiner Bock or Dos Equis, kick back, and learn it real good.

**Business Consultants**—read, enjoy, and then e-mail me at goalpath@att.net to discuss the requirements for becoming a MAS certified marketing alignment specialist.

**Industry Analysts**—regardless of how smart you think you are, check your ego at the door, and read this book cover to cover—you will gain knowledge that you can leverage in your own practice.

**Business Editors and Journalists**—I didn't major in English or Journalism, so don't expect *War and Peace*.

*To my lovely wife, Melanie,
without whose love, inspiration, and support
I would not have been able to write this book.*

# CONTENTS

## Chapter One – Marketing Alignment Overview
The view from 30,000 feet .................................................................. 1
Why does your company need Marketing Alignment? ......................... 5

## Chapter Two – The Elements of Marketing Alignment
Corporate Positioning ....................................................................... 15
Constantly Monitor Your Market's Dynamics .................................... 23
Product Line and Individual Value Propositions ................................ 24
Sales Channel Strategies .................................................................. 31
Messaging ........................................................................................ 33
Targeting .......................................................................................... 42
        Partners ............................................................................... 43
        Influencers .......................................................................... 48
        Customer and Market Segments .......................................... 52
Market Forces and Emerging Trends ................................................ 57
Tie it all together and you have Marketing Alignment! ...................... 59

## Chapter Three – Marketing Alignment and Corporate Success
Marketing Alignment and Corporate Survival .................................... 61
Intra-company Communications and Corporate Survival ................... 64
The Impact of Marketing Alignment on Corporate Success ............... 70

## Chapter Four – The Marketing Alignment Review Process
Internal vs. External Sourcing .......................................................... 73
The Marketing Alignment Review Process ....................................... 76
        Corporate Positioning ......................................................... 77
        Product Positioning and the Value Proposition .................... 80

| | |
|---|---|
| Sales Channel Strategies | 83 |
| Messaging | 87 |
|     Executive Messaging | 91 |
|     Advertising Messaging | 93 |
|     PR Messaging | 94 |
|     Sales and Partner Messaging | 96 |
|     Training Group Messaging | 102 |
|     Web Site Messaging | 103 |
| Targeting | 107 |
|     Targeting Customer Segments | 108 |
|     Targeting Channel Partners | 112 |
|     Targeting Total Product Solution Partners | 116 |
|     Targeting Influencers | 117 |
| The Overall Alignment Review Process | 123 |

## Chapter Five – The Marketing Alignment Remediation Process

| | |
|---|---|
| Start with the Strategic Elements | 129 |
|     The Corporate Positioning Statement | 129 |
|     Product Positioning and Value Propositions | 136 |
|     Sales Channel Strategies | 143 |
|     Messaging | 153 |
|         Executive Messaging | 154 |
|         Advertising Messaging | 156 |
|         Your PR Group and Messaging | 160 |
|         Your Sales Team and Messaging | 164 |
|         Your Training Group and Messaging | 167 |
|         Your Web site and Messaging | 168 |
|         Messaging and Remediation | 169 |
|     Targeting | 171 |
|         Customer Segment Targeting | 171 |
|         Partner Targeting | 175 |
|         Sales Channel Partner Targeting | 176 |
|         Total Solution Partner Targeting | 182 |
|         Influencer Targeting | 185 |
| Review, Analyze, and Compare – Again and Again | 190 |

## Chapter Six – Corporate Leadership and Marketing Alignment

| | |
|---|---|
| Bringing It All Together | 191 |

# CHAPTER ONE

# MARKETING ALIGNMENT OVERVIEW

## The view from 30,000 feet

Every day, companies across the globe disappear from radar while new ones emerge. Journalists and the media explain away this phenomenon using almost as many reasons for these failures as there are businesses failing: poor technology, bad management or mismanagement, inadequate marketing or advertising, poor customer service, product flaws, bad timing, anemic cash flow, economic downturns, etc. Of course, there are also those companies that seem to flourish regardless of the prevailing economic conditions, year after year, decade after decade. In fact, during downturns in their specific market sectors or in the overall economic environment, these companies tend to *gain* market share. How is that possible? Are they just lucky? Do they have the best engineers? The best management? The most efficient systems? Cutting-edge advertising campaigns? The most empowering corporate environment? Most likely, they benefit from most or all of these advantages, but that alone is not the primary secret to their survival. The secret is more about maintaining alignment of all of their efforts, most importantly sales and marketing alignment. This is what separates the great CEOs from the also-rans. Marketing alignment is a prerequisite for market leadership. It really doesn't matter if a company has world-class operations and people: if management doesn't see to it that all divisions and departments work in harmony and do so within the constraints of customer, influencer, and market requirements, the organization will not achieve its goals or leadership in its respective market or markets.

How does marketing alignment fit into this scheme? Marketing alignment is simply about aligning all of a company's sales and marketing efforts. It means matching your sales and marketing efforts with customer, influencer, and market expectations and requirements. And it is about maintaining consistency in corporate positioning, product positioning, product value propositions, sales channel strategies, company and product messaging, and market targeting. Corporate alignment and marketing alignment are similar in a number of ways to an orchestra. All sections of the orchestra have to work in harmony with each other or the result is not going to meet expectations. In the corporate world it is hardly different. In music, misalignment might result in some sour notes, unexpected solos as result of bad timing, maybe poor overall sound quality, and in general, just a bad performance. In the business world, it could mean Chapter Eleven. Not the best bullet point on a CEO's list of achievements. The continuity of corporate alignment and marketing alignment has to be maintained in the face of ongoing disruptive business, technology, economic and market changes. Whether these changes are obvious or subtle, the corporate machine has to make adjustments and realign during these transitions. It is crucial in maintaining market share and/or market leadership. If one division or department reacts to a significant event or change in the marketplace and the rest of the divisions don't adjust in a similar fashion, the corporate wheels will start to come loose. The key here is maintaining alignment within all divisions and departments in the face of dynamic market changes. After all, no markets are static.

The elements that make up marketing alignment are not new. However, marketing alignment as a methodology and an overall business process is new. Using the orchestra metaphor, let's examine how some companies get it and others don't even come close.

Imagine an orchestra that only gets together as a group for performances. The rest of the time, each section practices independently of the other sections. The orchestra's conductor does meet with the section leaders to set expectations and go over each group's contribution to the performance. So the section leaders do have a good understanding of what the conductor expects in terms of their contribution in performing each piece of music at the upcoming performance. If each section's leader is a virtuoso, as well as an accomplished teacher and conductor, then the quality of the performances will be good. However, if one of more of the section leaders are not particularly good at teaching or conducting, then the performances will be lacking and substandard. Only a unified effort that consistently meets expectations of its conductor and its targeted audiences will do if the orchestra expects to achieve regional or national recognition. How can the conductor achieve this unified effort and optimize every performance? By working with the group as a whole and seeing to it that each member and each section works in harmony with each other.

By the same token, if a company expects to achieve market leadership, it will have to unify its efforts and meet the expectations and requirements of its targeted market. For example, if the CEO of a company meets with management on a regular basis and does a terrific job of communicating to each member of management the strategy, the goals and the guidelines for their specific departments, then they will have a reasonable chance of success. In fact, if the CEO and every member of the management team are virtuosos in their respective fields, and are exceptional leaders, then the company could very well succeed and thrive during economic downturns. For this to happen, each member of management would have to clearly understand corporate and product positioning and ensure that every message their team broadcast would be in line with that positioning. They would also have to have the same information about current market conditions, as well as the latest data on customer, influencer, and market expectations and requirements. And under the leadership of this virtuoso CEO, each division or department will have to be moving in the same exact direction and embracing this same positioning, along with the same value propositions and channel strategies. But most companies do not have virtuosos playing every position in management. Even if the company has virtuoso executives, trying to ensure that they all work in harmony and alignment with each other can be a daunting task.

This is where marketing alignment comes into play. Through the implementation of the marketing alignment process, CEOs can ensure that there is alignment of all of the sales and marketing efforts, and every department is performing at its maximum potential and in concert with every other department's effort. Such a unified effort, one in harmony with the market's requirements, will ensure that the organization's revenue and market share are maximized, while at the same time reducing marketing costs as a percentage of revenue. Market leaders understand this concept and leverage it to maintain their leadership position.

So how does sales and marketing alignment work and why is it so important in achieving market leadership? Each and every day a company's product messages and images are communicated through sales materials, marketing materials, corporate presentations, partner presentations, or through third parties such as the press and the analysts. If these messages and images are not consistent, coherent, and compelling then they are not in alignment, and their effectiveness is diluted or negated. And no company can afford to waste their precious resources, regardless of the economic climate.

If the company's messaging, positioning, and/or channel strategies are not in line with the market's expectations they will not be effective and will waste precious resources. If they are not in line with the market influencer's expectations, then they will not be effective and will waste precious resources. If they are not in line with customer expectations and requirements, they will be ineffective and waste resources. Marketing Alignment is about ensuring that corporate positioning, product positioning, product differentiation, product value propositions, channel strategies, and targeting, as well as all messaging and literature content, are in alignment with each other and with market expectations. Figure 1 shows how each one of these sales and marketing elements must be in alignment with every other element, and must match up with both the targeted customers and the market influencer's expectations.

If any of these elements are out of alignment, then the company will be wasting marketing dollars and losing sales and market share. Sales revenue and market share are the lifeblood of any company. No CEO can afford to waste precious marketing dollars or lose market share. It is definitely a recipe for disaster. Even the best-managed companies cannot continue operations for very long if they are misdirecting their marketing efforts and losing market share. A market leader would not maintain its leadership position for very long if it were wasting its precious marketing resources. In a down economy, such behavior will only hasten the end.

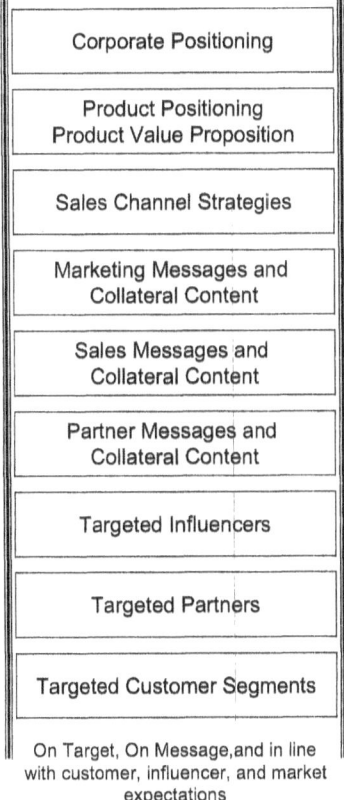

Figure 1
**The Elements of Marketing Alignment**
*Alignment means keeping all of these elements consistent with each other, and with market expectations and requirements*

- Corporate Positioning
- Product Positioning / Product Value Proposition
- Sales Channel Strategies
- Marketing Messages and Collateral Content
- Sales Messages and Collateral Content
- Partner Messages and Collateral Content
- Targeted Influencers
- Targeted Partners
- Targeted Customer Segments

On Target, On Message, and in line with customer, influencer, and market expectations

## *Why does your company need Marketing Alignment?*

Most companies began life with the creation of a mission statement and a corporate or strategic positioning statement. These statements should be separate and somewhat different, but they still have to be in alignment with each other. The mission statement has more to do with the organization's direction, vision, and values than the products or services the company offers. The corporate or strategic positioning statement (CPS or SPS) articulates what the company does, how it does it, how it is different, why it is better, and the company's overall value proposition. In fact, any company that cannot distill its corporate positioning statement into three sentences or less—preferably a single sentence—will not last very long. If it takes more verbiage than that to explain what a company does, then the company does not have a clear understanding of what it does. The company management will have to return to the drawing board and resolve this dilemma before they can move ahead with their business plan. The CPS is the cornerstone from which all company messaging is developed. It should be well thought out and convey a most compelling message if the company is to succeed. The corporate positioning statement should be unique and at the same time address the competitors within the market in which the company plans to compete. In addition, it has to be in alignment with the expectations of its chosen market or markets.

From the CPS, the company will develop product positioning and the individual value propositions for each product the company intends to offer. Product positioning is an integral part of the product message. Product positioning identifies the segment of the market that your product will be targeting. Identifying your competitors and articulating your differentiation from those competitors defines a product's position within its target market or market segment. Companies define the positioning of their products by identifying their competitors within their targeted markets. When a new company enters a market and claims to have no competition, it is most surely deluding itself. No competition means there is effectively no market in which to compete. There are exceptions to the rule. It is certainly possible for a new product to be spawned from a disruptive or revolutionary new technology. In that case, a new market can be created. The competitors will consist of the companies providing the old method of solving this problem, so there is competition. And keep in mind that it is extraordinarily expensive to educate customers and create a new market.

The larger a market is, the more competition there is in that market. The larger a market is, the larger the competitors are in both size and resources. Unless the new entrant's product has an overwhelming advantage over every one of the current offerings within that market, the new entrant should think twice about entering the larger overall market. It is always more prudent to select a small segment of the larger market when initially entering that market. The chances for survival are greater. Once a company establishes itself in the smaller market segment or niche, it can

## Chapter One: Marketing Alignment Overview

expand its market reach and grow its business accordingly. So, product positioning is primarily about the company choosing a specific market segment in which to launch its newest product. Ultimately, the targeted customers and influencers in that market segment will make the final determination about your product's specific positioning, so you would be well advised to choose a customer or market segment that will unanimously agree with your choice, buy into your positioning, and reward your market segment selection.

Value propositions relate to the product's application, its differentiation (a.k.a. advantages and benefits), and the targeted customers who will most benefit from using this product. For those readers in service industries, just simply substitute the term service where the term product is used, and the parallels should make sense. Service companies can and should follow the same path in developing value propositions and positioning for the services they intend to offer. The product value proposition is similar to the corporate positioning statement (CPS) in that it articulates what the product does, how it does it, why it is better, and who would gain the most benefit by using it. The value proposition must include a clearly defined differentiation statement. The primary differentiation is an undisputable claim about the product that the other competitors within the market segment cannot make. This statement has to create a must-have attitude in the mind of its targeted customers. If a company cannot create value proposition that includes such a claim, then that company's product will not be successful in the market for which it is targeted. The value proposition has to be in tune with the expectations of the customer, the influencer, and other market forces. The market's expectations are typically the expectations of the combined market forces—journalists, analysts, thought leaders, competitors—and the customer segments that make up the targeted market. The dominant market leading company will have a significant impact on market expectations. In fact, markets are a direct reflection of the customers, market influencers, and competitors within those markets. Each market is typically segmented by quality, price, functionality or capability, and the service or support requirements that are associated with the companies and products in that market.

From the well of the product value proposition flow marketing messages and sales messages. These messages must first of all be in line with each other, or market confusion will spring eternal from the very source from which they were born. Next, these messages have to articulate the value proposition in a manner that makes sense to the audiences targeted for consumption of the product or products. Messaging encompasses executive presentations, advertising copy, Web site content, sales and marketing literature and collateral, media releases and other presentation materials and copy, corporate financial and annual reports, corporate brochures and information packets, and any other content or copy that is broadcast by the company through the media or other mediums.

It is not uncommon for different departments within the company to create materials or presentations that do not follow corporate guidelines and are inconsistent with corporate or product positioning or value propositions. Consistency in style and format is also important in the context of marketing alignment. Typically, the most frequent offender in inconsistent messaging is the sales group. And, of course, they are the ones who need on-target, aligned messaging the most. There are numerous instances where sales team members create their own proposals, product data sheets, or competitive matrices, and do not follow corporate guidelines with regard to style, content, or product differentiation or positioning. There really must be someone responsible for monitoring and approving all content that is created inside and outside the company's marketing or creative group. Inconsistent messaging can cause confusion among the customers, influencers, and channel partners if not kept in check. This confusion will ultimately damage the image and reputation of the company, and will lead to lost revenue and market share, not to mention wasted marketing dollars. Alignment can prevent this.

It is critical that sales channel and distribution strategies are aligned with corporate and product positioning, as well as messaging. Sales channel strategies also have to coincide with influencer and customer requirements and expectations. This means that when the management team is establishing a channel strategy, sales and marketing management will have to come together and develop a sound channel strategy and recruit channel partners who target the same customer and market segments. The sales channel partners have to provide levels of service and support that meet both corporate guidelines and customer expectations. The sales approach of the channel partners must be in line with the corporate philosophy regarding corporate values and customer treatment. A training program will have to be developed and implemented to ensure proper tactics and consistent messaging by the channel partners. If a company expects to become a market leader, then it should choose its channel partners

Chapter One: Marketing Alignment Overview 9

accordingly. Whether a company sells directly or through distributors or resellers, the channel strategy must be in alignment with all other sales and marketing elements, and must meet customer and market expectations.

Finally, customer and influencer targeting must match corporate and product positioning. Because product positioning and the product value proposition define both market segment targets and specific customer types, this should not be an issue. However, misalignment in customer targeting has been known to occur during the development of marketing programs and/or in the selection of channel partners. Sometimes, new teams from different departments or divisions cause these types of alignment problems. As companies grow, managing and synchronizing sales and marketing efforts can become a daunting task. In other instances, there is no one responsible for making sure that sales and marketing efforts remain consistent with corporate direction and market expectations. This can be costly and can get a company started on the wrong foot. It is certainly not a prerequisite for market leadership.

Influencer targeting is about identifying journalists, analysts, and thought leaders who have the greatest influence on both product definition and customer buying decisions. These influencers can have a very significant impact on the success of products in the markets they cover. It is very important to gain a comprehensive understanding of the best practices and methodologies for developing strong and lasting relationships with these market influencers. In some industries and market segments, these influencers determine who the market leaders will be. Influencers can make or break companies simply by blessing or criticizing a particular product. Companies whose product's success is determined by their relative rankings in trade publications (as determined by editors, journalists, and analysts) had better be successful in developing relationships with these influencers or they will suffer the consequences. Editors and journalists do not need an introduction. In other markets, an analyst's recommendation can mean the difference between success and failure in that market. Some product successes are unaffected by these influencers, while others are greatly affected. Most executives and marketing managers have a good idea about the role specific market influencers play in a product's success.

Analysts, however, are not generally as well known as their journalist counterparts, and do require some explanation. Analysts work for analyst firms who cover industries such as technology, healthcare, financial services, manufacturing systems, pharmaceuticals, computers, automobiles, energy, communications, etc. Investment firms and the business media also retain analysts. Corporate buyers often consult with analyst firms during the buying decision process for guidance and direction. For example, a company that sells enterprise software to major corporations had better be recommended by the analysts covering this market or it will not even make the purchasing team's short list. It is extremely important that the product companies first identify the market makers—the top five or ten influencers—in their respective markets. Once they have identified these influencers, the next step is to develop relationships for the long run. The process of influencer identification and relationship building are both integral parts of the marketing alignment process. Building solid relationships with journalists and/or analysts does not happen overnight and requires a very specialized approach. Inexpensive consumer products are normally not affected by analysts or journalists in most instances.

The first step of marketing alignment is gaining a thorough understanding of the marketing alignment paradigm and the marketing alignment process. The next step is an initial marketing alignment review. This can be done by someone within the organization who has been appointed to be the marketing alignment coordinator, or by an outside consultant familiar with the marketing alignment review process. In either case, it is not something that should be undertaken casually. If market leadership is your primary objective, you will have to implement a marketing alignment program in your organization. Your company's success will depend on it.

Your sales and marketing efforts and programs should be reviewed, realigned, and monitored on an ongoing basis. Marketing alignment will not only ensure survival during uncertain business climates, it will contribute to revenue and market share growth in virtually any economic climate. Achieve true marketing alignment and not only will your revenue and market share increase, your marketing expenses, as a percentage of revenue, will decrease. By reading this book, you will gain a thorough understanding of marketing alignment. Chapter Two will discuss the elements of marketing alignment. Chapter Three will address marketing alignment and how it relates to corporate success. You will learn about the marketing alignment review process in Chapter Four. Chapter Five will tell you how to repair elements that are out of alignment and provide you with examples of companies that have done it right. Chapter Six provides a summation of the advantages and rewards of marketing alignment. In good economic times, a company can possibly survive or get by without marketing alignment, but it will never achieve significant growth or market leadership. Marketing alignment is the path to market leadership.

# Chapter Two

# The Elements of Marketing Alignment

Marketing alignment is critical to any company that sells or markets any product or service. It is essential if your goals are to keep your marketing expenditures in check, while at the same time growing market share and revenue. A number of books have been written about marketing, sales, and business development. Most of them offer sound advice and provide reasonably good insights on the best practices and proven methodologies required to succeed in the dynamic global markets of the twentieth and twenty-first centuries. However, up to this juncture, none of these publications have approached the subject of proper sales and marketing alignment.

Businesses are like machines. Each element of the organization has to perform at peak efficiency and work in harmony with every other element. To understand marketing alignment, first you will have to gain a clear understanding of each element of marketing alignment and its role in the marketing alignment paradigm. The elements of marketing alignment include corporate positioning, product positioning, product value propositions, sales channel strategies, messaging, and targeting. (*See Figure 1.*) When one or more of these elements moves out of alignment with the others or the expectations of the market, an organization's revenue growth and market leadership are limited. Additionally, the organization's ability to optimize its marketing efforts is restricted. (*See Figure 2.*)

This chapter will examine each of these elements and their relationship with each other and to overall company success.

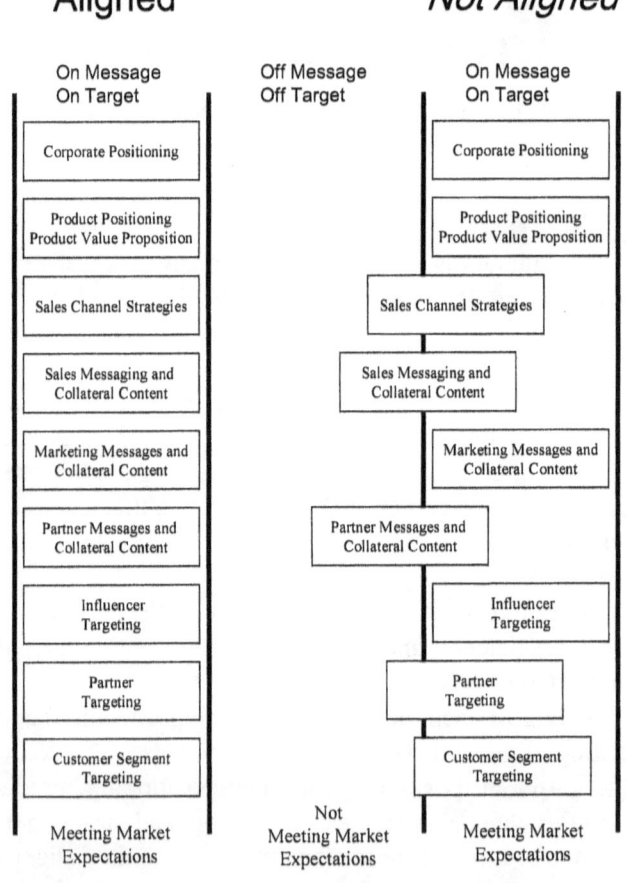

Figure 2
**Marketing Misalignment**
*When one or more of the marketing alignment elements move off target, off message, or no longer match customer, influencer, or market expectations, then <u>misalignment</u> occurs*

## Chapter Two: The Elements of Marketing Alignment

### *Corporate Positioning*

Most modern corporations create values statements, mission statements, and corporate positioning statements (CPS) for the purpose of describing their role and positioning within their specific markets. While it is important to create and distribute these philosophical and strategic guidelines to employees and the outside world, it is equally (if not more) important to ensure that they are continuously reviewed and updated. Markets are anything but static and given the rapid changes occurring in most markets, it is critical that companies continually evaluate their role and positioning in the marketplace to make sure that they remain in alignment with market expectations and ensure their competitive edge.

Values statements are a good place to start, given the confusion about their validity and just how sincere most organizations are in maintaining and enforcing the values stated in their values statements. To put it bluntly, values statements are of questionable value. Enron's values statement included words such as respect, integrity, excellence, and communication. What's wrong with this picture? In an article in the March 2002 issue of *Business 2.0*, Thomas A. Stewart suggested it would make more sense to issue a code of conduct rather than a values statement. Sort of a Ten Commandments for businesses—no stealing, no sexual harassment, no racism, no bribes, and so on.... It is my contention that if management was more conscientious and did a better job in hiring and partner selection in the first place, this problem could be eliminated on the front end. If you hire people with good values and sound judgment, then you will not need a values statement.

Mission statements, on the other hand, are certainly important in articulating corporate philosophy and setting the direction of the company. These statements are normally created during the initial startup stage of the organization. As the company grows and evolves, so should the mission statement. Mission statements are as different as the companies that create them. Who creates the statement, what it includes, and how it is structured have always been interpreted in a variety of ways. It would be difficult to argue that there is one correct way to develop this document. There are, however some basic fundamentals to which the majority of organizations adhere when crafting their mission statement. Christopher Bart, who has done extensive research on corporate mission statements, states:

"A good mission statement captures an organization's unique and enduring reason for being, and energizes stakeholders to pursue common goals. It also enables a focused allocation of organizational resources because it compels a firm to address some tough questions: What is our business? Why do we exist? What are we trying to accomplish?" (Bart, 98)

Mission statements should be short and go straight to point. One or two sentences will suffice. Simplicity is the key in this exercise. Very large corporations will typically have an overall corporate mission statement, as well as more specific individual mission statements for each division. A mission statement should be as simple or as complex as the organizations for which it is written. It should describe what the company does, the specific market in which it does this, and its proposed strategic advantage. A lot of companies will try to include values, visions, principles, and other information that does not really belong in a mission statement. We have already touched on values statements and their importance. Vision statements are valuable in their own right, but are not always incorporated into the mission statement. The vision statement is typically a future view of the organization, the internal environment it will create, and its impact on the community it serves and the market space in which it competes. It will include additional information about market direction, employee interests, and corporate culture. In most instances, the vision and mission statements are separate documents and are both very important to the organization. In some cases, the naming convention for this statement, vision or mission, is up to the individual corporation and its authors.

Mission statements vary greatly in length, scope, and format. Leo Burnett, a highly successful advertising agency, created a mission statement that is short and to the point: *The mission of Leo Burnett is to create superior advertising.* Cannondale, a leading U.S. manufacturer of bicycles, states: *Our passion is to be the best cycling and off-road motorsports company in the world. Our focus is people—employees, customers, retailers, and our vendors—working together to accomplish our mission.* The Cannondale mission statement goes on to explain how they intend to succeed, mentioning such things as producing a stream of innovative products while remaining lean, competitive, and entrepreneurial, concentrating on detail, continuously improving, and putting 90% of their profits back into the company. The mission statement is part of the Cannondale philosophy, which is approximately half a page in length. It should be mentioned that different companies employ a wide variety of methods and formats in articulating their mission or corporate philosophy.

Some companies place a higher emphasis on vision than mission and that is what you will find when you review their corporate literature or visit their websites. For example, Sun Microsystems, Inc. articulates their vision this way: *Since its inception in 1982, a singular vision—The Network is the Computer™ has propelled Sun Microsystems, Inc. (Nasdaq: SUNW) to its position as a leading provider of industrial-strength hardware, software, and services that power the Internet and allow companies worldwide to take their businesses to the nth. Sun can be found in more than 170 countries and on the World Wide Web.* This statement incorporates a combination of corporate history and mission into the vision statement. The point here is that it is important to identify where you are going and how you intend to get there. Mission or vision, it's all about semantics...but the most important point is that your company has one.

Who should author the mission statement? Most companies take the top down approach. The executive team architects the first few versions of the first draft. In some cases, one member of the executive team will craft the first draft of the document, then facilitate a consensus process with the rest of the management team to arrive at a final draft. Once the final draft is completed, it is distributed to the entire manager and employee population for comments, criticism, and suggestions for improvement. Remember, it's extremely important that those people responsible for performing the mission have a contribution in the final product. After all, they are part of the process and primary contributors to the success or failure of the organization. If you leave them out of the process, they will feel disenfranchised and will not be as effective in seeing that the company's mission is realized. The most effective method of employee empowerment is to involve them in the process every step of the way.

Employee involvement in the mission statement should not end with the final draft of the corporate mission statement. In order to ensure consistency of the mission and employee buy-in from the top down, each division or department should have its own mission statement, and all employees should be charged with creating their own personal mission statement relating to their role and contribution to the overall mission. Each mission statement should be prominently displayed in appropriate areas of the company offices in plain sight of both employees and visitors. Displaying these documents in prominent locations will go a long way in reinforcing and reminding the employees that they have an important role in fulfilling the company mission.

Continually reviewing and updating the mission statement is very important in maintaining proper corporate direction and market position. Cray Research's mission statement stated that the company's primary mission was to produce and distribute the world's fastest computer. Its commitment to its mission made it difficult for Cray to alter its direction as the technology and computer markets moved towards smaller, less expensive computers and computer networks. Consequently, they were displaced by smaller, nimbler organizations that were able to adjust their missions and reinvent themselves as the market evolved.

It is essential for the executive team to check their egos at the door and face the realities of the market place and its changing constitution. If they do not, then they very well might end up like the railroad companies. The railroad companies pigeonholed themselves in the railroad industry. They never saw the bigger picture. Their mission statements addressed market leadership in the railroad industry. If they would have come to the realization early on that they were in the transportation industry, not the railroad industry, they very well could have become global multinational conglomerates, instead of dying, government-subsidized shells of the industrial powerhouses they were five decades ago. They would have moved into air and ground transportation markets and solidified their positions. To sustain a market leadership position, companies have to maintain their forward vision of what the markets will bring.

While it is imperative to always know the company's mission, it is equally important to craft a corporate positioning statement. It should be noted that some companies combine their corporate positioning statement with their mission statement. It can be done, but I believe that the corporate positioning statement should be separate from the mission statement. While the mission statement speaks to what the company does and how it does it, the statement doesn't usually address how the company differentiates itself from its competitors or its value proposition.

## Chapter Two: The Elements of Marketing Alignment 19

Corporate or strategic positioning statements are all about what the company does, how it does this, how it does this differently from the competition, why it is better, and its value proposition. The value proposition is about competitive advantage. A company's competitive advantage should be intuitively obvious to potential customers. The acid test for a startup CEO has to do with being able to articulate corporate positioning in one or two sentences. This is also known as the "elevator statement." If the CEO or founder cannot articulate the corporate positioning statement in the time it takes to ride an elevator up or down a few floors (basically a minute or two), then he or she does not have a clear vision of what his or her company does and how it will succeed in the market. Venture capitalists routinely use a company's corporate positioning statement as one of the primary considerations for determining whether or not they should invest in that company.

If the company is a one-product company, then the corporate positioning statement should mirror the product positioning statement—what the product does, how it does it, how it is different, why it is better, and the value proposition. If the company is a multi-product company, the corporate positioning statement is more general in nature and reflects the overall market in which the company competes and its competitive advantage in that overall market. For the purpose of clarity, the following explanation of a corporate positioning statement will address a single-product company. In such a scenario, the company and product differentiation, along with the value proposition, will be the same. At the end of this discussion there will be an example comparing a multi-product company and single-product company and how their respective corporate positioning statements would differ.

Let's look at the individual components of the corporate positioning statement. *First, the statement addresses the business or market within which the company intends to compete.* If a company makes cars, obviously, it is in the car business. If the company produces toothbrushes, it is in the toothbrush or personal hygiene business. This is not normally a hard concept to understand or convey; however, when a company is creating a new market or business, it can be a daunting task trying to describe it to potential investors. An example of this is the Segway™ Personal Transportation vehicle invented by Dean Kamen, which debuted in 2001.

The product is an unusual-looking, gyro-balanced, battery-powered, two-wheeled personal transportation device. It looks more like a golf club pull-cart, the kind you would use if you wanted to walk, but didn't want to carry your clubs. So if you are Dean Kamen, how do you describe what business you are entering? You could call it the personal vehicle business, or the electric cart business, or maybe the personal intuitive transportation vehicle business. After all, it goes forward when you lean forward and goes backward when you lean backward. It is intuitive. Then again, the U.S. Post Office is testing these vehicles, so you could describe it as the personal commercial transportation small package conveyance.

Another more familiar market is the Post-it™ note market. Imagine how hard it must have been to pigeonhole those little sticky note pads into a market segment. Normally, defining your market should not be too difficult, but it can be if you are creating a market that did not exist before.

*The second component of the corporate positioning statement is how the company participates in the business.* After all, the company might be a supplier of services, parts, or raw materials for the product, rather than the maker of the product itself. A company might be in the yacht business and not build yachts. It could be the leading provider of anchors or motors. Generally, this should be a fairly simple exercise unless you are creating parts or components that heretofore did not exist. Another possibility is if your company manufactures parts, components, or systems that would revolutionize how a known product is built, assembled, or functions. In that case, it might require some wordsmithing to make the statement comprehensible. Normally, this description should be straightforward and not that difficult.

*The third component has to do with how your company differentiates itself.* This is a critical piece of the puzzle. To a large extent, differentiation will determine your company's success or failure in your chosen market. Solid differentiation requires that you are able to make an undisputable claim about your company and its products that your competitors cannot make. This claim has to represent a clear and significant benefit that will create a must-buy attitude in the mind of your targeted customers. This is particularly important if you intend to compete in an existing market dominated by a major company with a large percentage of market share. New Balance Athletic Shoe, Inc. has focused its corporate differentiation on building the best running shoes available and offering them in all widths and sizes. There are a number of other very good running shoes available, but these manufacturers have tended to offer a more limited variety of sizes and widths. In most cases, New Balance's competitors have opted for wider distribution channels and offered fewer size and width options through these channels.

Nike's meteoric growth and popularity, which began with the introduction of an innovative line of high tech running shoes, has been leveraged by Nike to expand its product offerings to include apparel, golf clubs, miscellaneous sports equipment, and other athletic accessories. Nike has based its positioning on endorsement contracts with major sports superstars along with its "Just Do It" advertising campaign to build worldwide brand identification. The company has built brand equity to the point where Nike's major differentiation today is its brand and its continuing association with the world's greatest athletes. "Let me grab my Nikes and we will go running or play tennis, etc." Only companies that have become dominant market leaders can use brand equity as their differentiation, and even then they still have to offer innovative, cutting-edge products to sustain their momentum.

There is another method of differentiation besides product superiority. That method of differentiation is pricing. For me-too products—those products that offer no clear competitive advantage—pricing is the only way to differentiate. This occurs typically when a product category reaches the commodity status. This product will adhere to standard specifications and the product life cycle has achieved mainstream status with no expected product changes or innovation in the near term expected.

Understand that a company that takes this approach is always at the mercy of market dynamics—namely, a competitor launching an enhanced version of the me-too product. There are generally very slim profit margins that expose the me-too companies to the market leader's efficiencies of scale, not to mention their brand recognition advantages. Examples of this phenomenon are abundant. Generic or store brand items in grocery store chains are excellent examples. So-called clone personal computers are another example. What's interesting about this phenomenon is that in a number of instances the market leading companies produce the unbranded products in the same factories as those with the name brands. This is usually more common among consumer product companies than companies producing the more expensive, big-ticket items. However, it is common in business-to-business companies as well.

*The final component of the corporate positioning statement is the value proposition.* The value proposition ties together the overall applications for which your company's products will be used, along with your company's differentiating factors and targeted market segments. Unless a company is highly diversified like GE, the company and its product lines should be closely connected. The company's value proposition and its product's value propositions should be almost identical. The product's application identifies exactly how and for what purpose the product will be used. In determining the value proposition, the company will have to validate which product benefits are most important to the target market segment. As an example of a value proposition, a Lexus RX 300 value proposition might be articulated as follows: The Lexus RX 300 is a sports utility vehicle offering uncompromising luxury, safety, performance, comfort, and unparalleled customer service that will appeal to the upper end of the SUV market segment (income range of $75K+). Lexus is a market leader in the luxury car market and its corporate value proposition is the same as the value propositions for each of its vehicle models.

As previously stated, there is a difference between corporate positioning statements for single-product companies and multi-product companies. For example, if Microsoft only produced its office software suite, it might state that it was in the office productivity software business, that it offered a suite of productivity software including a spreadsheet, word processor, presentation software, database software, and project management software. Microsoft could further claim that it was different from the other productivity suites by virtue of its seamless integration, increased functionality, multi-user capabilities, and its incredibly large installed base of users. Its value proposition would be that it offers the only suite providing such a comprehensive set of features, the largest installed base, and that it is considered the industry standard. Since Microsoft offers a lot more than just productivity software suites, its corporate positioning is more about being the leading provider of all types of software. It differentiates itself by being the industry standard. Its value proposition is that it is the corporate standard and all of its products seamlessly integrate with each other.

The corporate positioning statement sets the tone and lays the foundation for all other company and product messaging. Because of the importance of the corporate positioning statement, it is imperative that it is conceived through a process involving the consensus of the executive team and a thorough understanding of company and product advantages and benefits, the competitive climate, market and influencer expectations, and the company's vision. This is not an exercise that should be taken

Chapter Two: The Elements of Marketing Alignment    23

lightly. Marshal all available company forces to carry out this process. This applies to the continual review and update process as well.

## *Constantly Monitor your Market's Dynamics*

It has never been more important to continuously monitor market dynamics than it is today. Due to the technological advances in rapid product development, just-in-time manufacturing, and light speed communication transmission, markets can change overnight. Everyone in the company should include monitoring market dynamics as part of their job description. Look for such things as changes in customer and influencer expectations, market-changing events or announcements, and emerging new product trends. Updates to the corporate positioning statement should coincide with major changes in the market.

Obviously, it does not make sense to rewrite this document too frequently, especially when you consider the fact that these changes will impact every other piece of sales and marketing collateral produced by the company. On the other hand, if the corporate positioning statement does not reflect current market conditions and expectations, then neither will any of the other company literature or presentations. This in turn will lead to ineffective marketing and lost revenue. Changing market conditions will not occur every other month or necessarily every six months. Generally, you can expect changes to occur every one or two years. These market dynamics will most likely accelerate in the coming years. In most cases, only subtle changes to the document will be required. Common sense will dictate what needs to be changed and when these changes should take place, and then they can be undertaken accordingly.

Novell, the Provo, Utah network software vendor, owned the networking market in the early 90s, but misjudged the importance of the Internet. Consequently, their corporate and product positioning did not change as the Internet began to emerge as the primary global communications backbone. The company's fortunes began a reversal that they have yet to overcome. Given the fact that the Internet has become the de facto network backbone in the computer world, it should have been apparent that it would impact Novell's business, but somehow they missed it. Microsoft was late in recognizing the importance of the Internet, but when they did finally come to the realization of just how seriously it was going to impact their business model, Bill Gates and his executive staff turned the company on a dime and redirected all of their efforts to embrace the Internet. Needless to say, they successfully dodged that bullet and have maintained their market leadership position. The longer it takes a company to recognize an emerging market or competitive force impacting their business, the more dramatically the company will have to react if it expects to maintain market share and/or market leadership. Vigilance is the key.

## *Product Positioning and Product Value Propositions*

Product positioning is similar to corporate positioning. Product positioning is all about what the product does, how it does it, why it is better than the competitors' product, how it is different from the competitors' product, and what its value proposition is all about. Product positioning is about a product's position in the market place and how it stacks up against its competition. To a certain extent, the product value proposition will determine a product's position in the market. After all, the value proposition addresses the product's application and the targeted customers who would most benefit from its use. The product's differentiation is also a part of the positioning equation. Product positioning is about targeting your competitors and the market segment in which you want to compete. In reality, its competitors, customers, and the market influencers define a product's position in the market. If a product company tells you it has no competition, then that company is deluding itself, because where there is no competition, generally, there is no market. It is possible that a new product's approach to solving a particular problem is unique and that is why the company doesn't believe it has any competition. However, the competition for that product is the older, more traditional method of solving the problem, and that does normally involve existing products.

When Intuit's *Quicken* entered the personal financial software market, they did not compete with other financial software companies. At that point in time, there were not any personal financial software products. They competed with the old-fashioned method of checkbook entries and reconciliation. The products involved in that process were a pencil, a check register, a calculator, and some writing paper. Their competition was more about changing personal habits than pointing to an existing competitor. So did they have competition? Sure, but it was more difficult to identify because the product competitors did not really compete in this

## Chapter Two: The Elements of Marketing Alignment      25

new market. Yes, they did compete against the companies that marketed pencils, calculators, and check registers, but in an indirect manner. The problem in a market where there is effectively no true head-to-head competition, other than an old-fashioned process or method, is that the company involved will have to spend a great deal of time and resources educating this new market about their new method or technology. Intuit was successful in educating this market and has been able to maintain its market leadership position against some formidable competitors, including Microsoft.

Typically, in existing markets, there are low-end, mid-range, and high-end components of the market. As markets mature and grow, they become more segmented. For example, in the automobile market there are literally dozens of segments. There are mini, sub-compact and compact economy cars; there are small, mid-size, and large luxury cars; there are small, mid-size, and large touring sedans; there are small, mid-size, and large sport coupes; there are small, mid-size, and large sports utility vehicles; there are small, mid-size, large, very large and even gigantic trucks; there are sports cars that range from small economy types to ultra, high performance and exotic...and on and on and on. So positioning is really more about your competitors than it is about your value proposition and differentiation.

Positioning is your relative position in the market space. Your company will initially define the market segment where it expects its products will compete. The market will then validate or invalidate that positioning. The market is comprised of your targeted customers, the market influencers and prognosticators, and your competitors. So, in effect, when you identify your competitors to the market, you're stating how and where you are positioned within that market. The seasoned competitors in any market have already established their position in that market, and by lining your company up against these established competitors you will have determined your initial market positioning. It is then up to the market to validate or invalidate your positioning.

The product value proposition is sometimes a misunderstood concept. As mentioned in the previous section, the value proposition addresses the product's differentiation or competitive advantage, its application, and the intended target market. More often than not, it is poorly researched and/or incorrectly validated prior to being established as the product's primary mantra. As outlined in Geoff Moore's book on technology marketing,

*Crossing the Chasm*, the value proposition creation process begins with the development of a two-dimensional matrix (think spreadsheet) that includes various applications or uses for the product on one axis, and the most likely target customer audiences on the other axis. Figure 3 is an example of a value proposition matrix for a cellular phone that also provides Internet access. Once the matrix is constructed, values will be assigned to each application/target market box in the matrix to determine which applications would be most compelling for each audience. Once those application/target market groups with the highest values are selected, it is time to research the competitors to determine what, if any, advantage your product has over the current competition for that application in that market segment. Let's examine each of the value proposition elements and identify each element's role in the value proposition creation process.

**Figure 3** – Sample Value Proposition Matrix for Cellular Phone with Internet Access

| Target Customer | Application | | | |
|---|---|---|---|---|
| | Check Stocks | Check E-mail | Check Inventory | Check Order Status |
| Business Traveler | 3 | 4 | 1 | 2 |
| Outside Sales Rep | 2 | 4 | 4 | 4 |
| Tech Support Rep | 2 | 4 | 1 | 1 |
| CEO | 3 | 4 | 2 | 2 |
| Other possible target customers | | | | |

As stated by Geoff Moore in his book, *Crossing the Chasm*, the rating system could be one through five with the following value assignments:

1. Not usable
2. Usable, but with no obvious benefits
3. Nice to have—the end user will appreciate these benefits although they are not strategic to the organization sponsoring the purchase
4. Should have—the end user receives strategic benefits, although these benefits can readily be achieved by other means as well
5. Must have—the end user receives benefits that are strategic to the sponsoring organization and cannot be achieved by any other reasonable means

Differentiation is the your product's competitive advantage. Given the enormous amount of information being disseminated over the airwaves, television, and the Internet, getting through the noise or buzz to deliver your product message is exceedingly difficult. If your product message is no different from that of your fellow competitors, or just a watered down version of theirs, then your company's chances of connecting with potential customers is diminished significantly. That's why it is so important to tell a better, more compelling story than your competitors to your target audience. Your differentiation or competitive advantage has to create a must-buy attitude in the mind of your targeted customer group.

In the example in Figure 3, if several phones offered e-mail messaging, the winner would probably be the phone with additional features that enhanced the e-mail function, such as a larger LCD screen, a color display, better graphics, more memory, etc. The most compelling feature group would have to be borne out through thorough market research and customer surveys. Once the new value proposition was validated and the product was configured accordingly, then the go-to-market strategy could be developed and implemented.

An example of superior differentiation was the HP Laserjet™ printer. Hewlett Packard was not a dominant force in the printer market prior to introducing its Laserjet. Epson was the market leader with its dot matrix line of printers. Epson had set the standard for microcomputer printers and had been the market leader for several years prior to HP's introduction of the Laserjet™. The laser printer technology, which, by the way, HP licensed from Canon, was far superior in both speed and quality. These were benefits that the business printer market clearly needed and wanted. Even though the laser printers were considerably more expensive and bulky, their speed and quality advantages far outweighed these disadvantages. The laser printer's advantages and benefits immediately created a must-buy attitude in the minds of the business consumers in this market segment.

Interestingly enough, Apple introduced a laser printer, the Apple Laserwriter, at about the same time. However, even though Apple's laser printers were designed to easily connect to Apple computers, they were not easy to connect to the industry standard PCs. There were a number of compatibility issues associated with Apple's laser printers. So the PC users opted to go with HP's laser printers. Consequently, HP has become the market leader in the printer market. In fact, they continue to take advantage of their market leadership position by continuing to innovate, add value, and develop products required by each segment of the PC printer market. HP currently has the lion's share of both the low-end and mid-range printer markets. Canon did not recognize just how huge the laser printer's differentiation advantage was going to be, and they allowed HP to capitalize on it even though Canon had pioneered this technology and could have become the market leading printer manufacturer. Canon has obviously made a great deal of money from the licensing fees, but just think how much more they could have made had they been the primary manufacturer.

So how does one go about finding a product's competitive advantage? In most cases, the company already has a vision of the product's competitive advantage prior to even beginning the product development. This is typically determined during product conception (i.e. we can build a better mousetrap with features X, Y, Z). This is not always the case, but it is in most cases. So if you know your product's competitive advantage, then why worry about the value proposition. It's a slam-dunk, right? Wrong. A number of things can happen during product development. The competition can introduce a new and improved widget during this time. The product development team can run into some insurmountable problems during development, changing the product either slightly or significantly. Complementary products or services might alter the most desirable type of product configuration for your intended market.

Let's just assume those events haven't occurred and move forward to the validation aspect of the product value proposition. In most instances you can do this because most of these issues will emerge during the validation process. Really, the only issue that might not be uncovered during validation is your company's inability to build to the proposed specifications.

So how does one validate a value proposition? Hire a psychic? Consult an astrologer! Have a tarot reading? Au contraire! Actually, the best way is to combine some in-depth market research with a survey of potential customers. You could also arrange for a focus group, but surveying potential customers is more reliable and provides a higher level of accuracy.

Market research should begin by analyzing your potential competitors. First, flesh out the top four or five market share leaders in your intended market. Review and analyze their target markets, their applications, their stated competitive advantages, their distribution and channel strategies and tactics, their advertising vehicles and messages, their sales approach, and what the analysts, journalists, and thought leaders have to say about their companies and their products. Once you understand your competitors inside and out, then you can determine your true competitive advantage or advantages. Document all pertinent competitor data along with similarities and differences between each of them. Then compare your value proposition to theirs and determine if, in fact, you can make your value proposition more compelling and beneficial to the target audience.

After completing the first segment of your market research, it's time to test your value proposition on the intended targeted customers. You can use telephone surveys, mail surveys, web surveys, or any combination of the three. The secret here is to ensure you pinpoint the right audience and you have a good method for tabulating the results. This generally means that you will have to design a survey that uses objective survey questions that can be tabulated in a minimal time and with minimal effort. The survey should not be over fifteen or twenty questions. If it is longer, the intended respondent will be less likely to complete the survey.

The survey questions should poll the respondents on how they are currently using your competitor's products, what they like and don't like about those products, what enhancements they would like to see made to those products, the nature of their shopping habits, how the products should be priced, the primary factors that impact their purchasing decisions, how they research these products, what publications or internet sites they rely on for their product information, and what other outside influences or influencers they used in making the buying decision. At the end of the survey, you could include a one paragraph description of your proposed offering and then ask them: "After reading this description, would you buy this product if it were available today?" Make sure that you get a large enough audience sample to validate your value proposition. Depending on your projected market size, 500 to 3,000 respondents should suffice. Regardless of the survey vehicle (mail, telephone, or your Web site) you will most likely have to use an incentive to guarantee a reasonable response. Examples of incentives are small gift items—pen sets, small calculators, micro clocks, etc.—or something like a gift certificate for a fast food meal or a movie. Typical direct mail response rates are two percent of the mailing; however, when a premium or incentive is included, the response rate can increase to 50%!

If you are thinking that this market research and customer survey is not necessary because you have no competition, then chances are you have no market, either. If there were an existing market, then you would certainly have competition. If no market has been created for your product, then you will have to spend a large fortune educating your intended customer base on the advantages of a product or offering for which they have not determined a need. Spending a large fortune to make a small fortune is not exactly a sound business practice. It is always better to alter your approach in targeting to include some credible competition. It's all about how you spin your offering's application and benefits. Typically, in such a scenario, the market does exist; it's just being served by a different kind of solution. So you will have to articulate a new and better way of solving the potential customer's problem. Otherwise, you will have to educate not just your prospective customers, but also the journalists, the industry analysts, and the thought leaders in the larger overall market space in which your new market segment would be included.

There are also instances in which it is best to target a niche in the larger market you are planning to enter. That way you can dominate the smaller segment first, then go after additional segments until you gain a reasonable share of the overall market. This is sometimes less expensive and a better business decision than going up against the market leader who already has brand equity and considerably more resources than your startup or smaller company. This is more of a back door approach and allows your company to come into the market under the behemoth's radar. There have been companies that have taken this approach and grown into $100M corporations before the market leader or leaders took any retaliatory action against the smaller entity.

Remember, the product value proposition has to include an indisputable statement about the product's primary advantage that no other competitor can make. This competitive advantage has to create a must-buy attitude in the targeted customer's mind. It has to be validated through market research and a survey of a reasonable sample of the target audience for this product. Once that is complete, then you can proceed to developing a go-to-market strategy and a product launch plan.

## Sales Channel Strategies

Different companies use different sales channel strategies based on the customer and market requirements for the products they sell. Sales channel and distribution strategies have to align with corporate and product positioning as well as messaging, and have to coincide with influencer and customer requirements and expectations. This means that when establishing a channel strategy, sales and marketing management will have to come together and develop a sound channel strategy that will engage channel partners who target the same customer and market segments, and provide levels of service and support that meet both corporate guidelines and customer expectations. It also means that the sales approach of the company's channel partners must be in line with its philosophy of customer acquisition and retention. The best way for your company to ensure that its channel partners follow corporate guidelines with regard to an acceptable sales approach, messaging, value proposition articulation, service, and after-sales support is to require that your channel partners undergo a comprehensive training program that teaches them proper tactics and consistent messaging techniques. If a company expects to become a market leader, then it should choose its channel partners accordingly. Channel partner targeting and selection will be discussed in more detail in the section of this chapter on targeting.

What is a sales channel strategy? Every company uses a sales force to sell its products to the customer groups or segments that the company targets. If your company sells green beans, then most likely you either sell them direct from a vegetable stand on the side of the road, or you use a reseller, such as a grocery store. If your company manufactures and sells automobiles then you develop a network of car dealers who can provide service and parts, as well as the sales facilities to sell the automobiles your company produces. If you sell rocket engines to N.A.S.A., chances are you have an in-house sales force that calls directly on the people responsible for selecting the rocket engine vendors and those decision makers who make the final buying decision. The sales channel is basically the infrastructure that is put in place to move products from the manufacturer to the final customer. The sales channel strategy involves first determining the structure, and then selecting the sales force. The sales force can come from inside the company or from organizations outside the company. The layers of organizations through which a product moves prior to reaching its final destination, i.e. the customer, determine the sales channel structure and strategy a company will use in distributing its products.

More complex product offerings, such as rocket engines, corporate information systems, jet airliners, manufacturing systems, etc. are typically sold directly by salespersons employed by the manufacturer. Less complex products, such as groceries, cosmetics, over-the-counter drugs, toys, clothes, and appliances are typically sold by third party retail organizations such as stores, shops, and mass merchandisers. Depending on the product category, middlemen such as wholesalers and distributors can also be involved in the sales channel structure. Sales channel strategies are normally set based on the price and complexity of the product. They are generally set to match the channel strategies of the other competitors within that market space.

There are manufacturers who have gone against conventional wisdom and have successfully developed unconventional channel structures through which to distribute their products. Before Dell Computer began using direct sales techniques to sell personal computers, PCs were sold primarily through computer stores. Now Dell is the number one manufacturer and marketer of personal computers in the world. They actually started out selling their PCs using mail-order and telesales channel methods, and later went on to become the first PC company to fully embrace the Internet as their primary sales channel. Dell overcame a number of formidable obstacles in revising the sales channel model for PC manufacturers to include custom configuration, localized service and support, and quick turnaround and fulfillment of customized PC orders. Traditional sales channel models used by your competitors should not necessarily be the only model that your company evaluates in determining the proper channel strategy. There have been numerous companies that have defied conventional wisdom and became market leaders by developing new, innovative channel models.

Developing a proper channel strategy is the first step in building a strong, successful sales channel. Where does management begin in developing this strategy? A good starting point is researching the channel distribution strategies of your competitors. Compare the market leader's channel strategies against those of the other leading competitors in the market segments your company plans to enter. Analyze the pros and cons of each model and see if one model is more appropriate than another for your company and your product positioning strategy. Think outside the box, as well, and see if there might be a better distribution method for your products.

Whatever strategy you choose has to be in alignment with your product's value proposition and your targeted customer segment's expectations. Does it make more sense to sell direct or use resellers? Should wholesalers or distributors be included in the structure? How will your proposed channel structure be embraced by the market influencers? How effective will your channel partners be in communicating your value proposition? How will your proposed strategy impact the cost of your products and the cost of sales? How effective will your channel partners be in helping your company move towards market leadership? How receptive will your targeted channel partners be in taking on your product, or products, or product lines? These are all questions that will have to be answered prior to setting your channel strategy. Partner selection will also be critical to the success of your company and its products. As mentioned earlier, channel partner selection is covered in the upcoming section on targeting in this chapter. Sales channel strategy and partner selection go hand in hand. However, you cannot begin the selection process until you have settled on your sales channel strategy.

## *Messaging*

Messaging encompasses virtually all communications emanating from the company's internal departments and messages that are broadcast by external sources such as market influencers. Messaging includes messages and presentations originating from your company's investor relations group, management, finance, marketing, public relations, sales, customer service, customer support, channel partners, strategic partners, and third parties such as journalists, analysts, and thought leaders. All messages should represent the company's mission, positioning, value proposition, values, and strengths in the best possible light and be consistent with each other as well as with customer, influencer, and market expectations. Inconsistent or misstated messaging is a common problem with even the best-managed and run companies in the world. The most common reason for problems with company messaging has to do with poor communication and the fact that no one in the company has been assigned responsibility for messaging management.

Since companies have many different organizational structures and responsibility hierarchies, it is difficult to pinpoint exactly what position would be responsible for ensuring message consistency and content. In some companies it could be the Vice President of Sales and Marketing, the PR Director or Manager, the Product Manager, or even the CEO, depending on company size. The actual person or persons who will review company messaging for consistency, clarity, and alignment will also depend on the size of the company and the size of the task. The most important issue here is that someone is given the responsibility and that person outlines exactly how he or she will go about managing this effort to all the parties involved. If at all possible, it would be best to establish a new position, a *marketing alignment coordinator*, to manage this function and other alignment functions. Bringing everyone involved together to discuss this issue and how it can be effectively managed is the best place to start. It is absolutely essential that the person with overall responsibility for company messaging communicate frequently with inter-company department heads and personnel, as well as intra-company groups and partners.

Company messaging is the responsibility of a number of groups within the company. Typically, it begins with product management and marketing. Keep in mind that product management and marketing groups are organized quite differently from one company to the next, and have different functional responsibilities based on their organizational structures. One operational philosophy that is relatively consistent across most organizations is the role of product management in developing the value proposition and the basic message of each product or product line. In well-managed organizations, this value proposition and basic message is developed after thorough market research and is based on perceived customer, influencer, and market requirements. While the product management group conceives the value proposition and the basic product message, the final drafts of these documents are the responsibility of the marketing or product marketing team. In organizations where product management drives all aspects of the product life cycle, all marketing programs and messages fall under the direction of the product manager. In other company structures, the marketing function would be in a separate department or group. In either case, all marketing messages should be consistent with the company mission, company positioning, and customer, influencer, and market expectations and requirements.

## Chapter Two: The Elements of Marketing Alignment 35

Marketing messages include advertising, brochures, data sheets, customer success stories, white papers, online demos, logos, and other corporate or product images, Web site content, package copy and content, promotional content, and all company presentations. In some cases, the vendor company's marketing group creates partner presentations and collateral materials. There are also instances where the marketing group will subcontract advertising copy, images, custom content such as white papers, case studies, customer success stories, promotional writing, or other promotional content or images. In each case, these pieces should be checked carefully for content consistency and accuracy as it relates to the product or company positioning, differentiation, and value proposition.

In different organizations, press relations or public relations (PR) is either part of marketing or an entire department separate from marketing. This is also true of analyst relations (AR). In some industries and markets, the analysts play as significant a role in influencing customer-buying decisions as do journalists in other markets. For most vendors selling to the Fortune 500 companies, being blessed by the analysts determines whether a vendor even gets consideration. It's life or death for these companies, so ensuring both message consistency and meeting the analysts' expectations is critical. It is very important that the marketing group or the marketing alignment coordinator evaluate the consistency, clarity, and coherence of any messaging or presentations that are created by the PR or AR groups. In some companies, these organizations disseminate a tremendous amount of information to the media and analyst communities, so the task can be daunting for the marketing group or marketing alignment coordinator. The same standards apply: consistency and accuracy in relating to the company and product positioning, differentiation, and value proposition in accordance with customer, influencer, and market expectations and requirements.

This means that the first organizational areas where inconsistent product messaging is likely to occur is in product management, marketing, PR, and AR. If the product management group drives marketing, AR, and PR, then it's up to the product management director or the newly assigned marketing alignment coordinator to monitor the consistency and clarity of all of these messages. Therefore, the first area that the marketing alignment coordinator should focus on with regard to messaging consistency is communication between the product management and marketing groups. It might seem that if there is, indeed, a marketing alignment coordinator then his or her first responsibility should be ensuring consistency between the corporate mission statement, the corporate positioning statement, and the corporate value proposition and customer, influencer, and market expectations and requirements. Of course, since corporate positioning is typically set by the CEO and senior management team, the marketing alignment coordinator will have to exercise a modicum of diplomacy and tact in suggesting changes or modifications to these individual creations of senior management. After all, they are, in effect, the organization's Holy Grail. In reality, the CEO should be quite receptive to any suggestions from the marketing alignment coordinator since the CEO most likely created this position and handpicked the person to fill it. In really small organizations, the CEO could assume the role of the marketing alignment coordinator.

Next, let's look at the sales, customer service, and customer support groups. Why would the messages coming from any of these groups be different from those messages emanating from the marketing department? During the early stages of development or evolution of an organization, the sales and marketing functions are typically combined. Later, as the company grows, they become completely separate sub-organizations within the company. It's not uncommon for these individual departments within the organization to evolve like mini-fiefdoms and not only enjoy their independence from the other departments, but overdo this newfound independence. These independent entities will do such things as create their own collateral materials and a somewhat different approach to articulating the product positioning or differentiation.

This happens when the sales group believes it has a clearer understanding of customer expectations and requirements, and can better articulate this knowledge into a more compelling value proposition. Even if this is true, the sales group must communicate this new knowledge to the marketing group or marketing will continue to disseminate its original message while sales broadcasts a different message. In a number of companies, the sales organization is responsible for creating their own sales collateral materials. Even if the sales group does not create collateral materials, they are probably creating sales proposals or the verbal equivalent—the sales pitch. Through these proposals or pitches the sales group is still capable of sending inconsistent, incompatible messages to potential customers. The result is message inconsistency that will only escalate market confusion and reduce sales revenue and market share. Internal

## Chapter Two: The Elements of Marketing Alignment    37

miscommunication can bring down a company if it becomes too pervasive. This is a situation where a marketing alignment coordinator could intervene and nip this type of problem in the bud.

While working as a product manager at Computer Associates in 1988, I witnessed this phenomenon first-hand. The product lines I managed were the low-end and mid-range accounting software applications for microcomputers. At that time, Computer Associates offered low-end, mid-range, and high-end accounting software for microcomputers. Our low-end line consisted of a PC compatible product and a product for Apple Computer's recently introduced Macintosh. The PC product was developed in-house, and the Macintosh product was developed by a third party developer out of Phoenix. The two products had a number of similarities, but they were quite different in many areas. The Macintosh product was much more user friendly and had a typical Macintosh graphic user interface—very intuitive and easy to use. The PC version did not have a graphic user interface. One or two of our dealer account managers represented these products to our dealers as being identical in look and feel as well as functionality, capacities, and capabilities. This was simply not true and caused some friction between CA and our authorized dealer group.

Once I got wind of what was going on, I immediately addressed the problem and got our sales reps' presentations aligned with the actual positioning and product details for each of these products. It could have gotten ugly and disenfranchised some of our best performing dealers had we not identified the problem and resolved it quickly. At that time, the outside dealer reps were dispersed across the U.S. and did not get together with the product group more than a couple of times per year. Some of the account reps actively communicated with the product group and did not encounter these problems. Unfortunately, there were some who did not. Who was at fault? The blame fell on both sides. Had there been a communication briefing system in place, these types of problems could have been avoided. Communications between product management, marketing, and sales is critical to the alignment process.

In some companies, the customer service and customer support groups are a part of the sales organization, and in other companies they are separate entities within the overall organization. Regardless of the organizational structure, they can impact messaging in a similar manner, as can the sales group. Most companies provide these groups with the ability to sell additional products or services to the customer during the course of a customer service or support call. In many instances, the customer service or support person is the first contact a customer has with an employee from the product manufacturer.

This is particularly true when the vendor's products are sold through resellers, distributors, integrators, or other third party distribution channels. If this is the case, it is doubly important that this first communication include a clear, concise articulation of the company mission, position, and message during the conversation between the company service person and the customer. This is an excellent opportunity for the company to accurately broadcast a consistent message that is in alignment with its other messages and customer, influencer, and market expectations. For those companies that believe customer retention is critical to their longevity and ultimate survival, it doesn't take a rocket scientist to ascertain the importance of these communications. A marketing alignment coordinator would be able to review these operations and make recommendations on how to improve these communications.

It is probably safe to assume that everyone reading this book has come across a customer service or support person who has misrepresented their company's product, or represented their company in a negative manner. Possibly these customer service folks were rude, or offered no help whatsoever. How do you suppose that reflects on the company's image, its products, or the employees of that company? If part of the company's value proposition is customer service, then that message will be lost, as well as the company's alignment with that part of its overall value proposition. If the value proposition for a company's product is reliability and quality, and the product is dead on arrival at the customer's door, you can kiss the validity of that message goodbye. Customers should be your company's most valuable assets. Your company's customer service has to match your customer service message.

Recently, I purchased a portable CD burner for my laptop through an Internet vendor that sells products refurbished by the respective manufacturers. When I went to install this device on my laptop, I discovered that the installation software provided with the unit was not compatible with the latest version of Microsoft Windows. The manufacturer's customer service person explained to me that his company had no plans to offer a Windows 2000 compatible version of the software for this burner. He went on to say that if I wanted to use my new CD burner, I would have to

## Chapter Two: The Elements of Marketing Alignment 39

spend an additional $80.00 with a third party software vendor who in fact had a more recent version of the software that was compatible with my operating system. That was the first straw. The burner worked for about six months and then died. The product was represented as having a one-year manufacturer's warranty from the date of purchase. The manufacturer's representatives insisted that the product's warranty had expired even though I had owned it for only six months. After a myriad of emails and conversations with more customer service persons, I was allowed to send back my dead unit. Two months later I received the replacement unit. Guess what? It worked for about an hour before it cratered. How much business do you think I will be doing with that company in the future? None! It should also be mentioned that this same manufacturer describes itself as "...a global leader in reliable portable storage systems." Does this sound like an alignment problem? You bet. The company shall remain nameless, which will probably be its destiny if its management does not update the company's current strategy and their products, and reevaluate their service policies.

Where do partners and messaging enter into this equation? Sales channel partners are extensions of your sales and marketing organizations. If your company sells its products or services through third party channels such as dealers, resellers, distributors, product integrators, or other sales channel partners, then those organizations and their personnel are directly representing your company and your products to potential customers. Whether you like it or not, their messaging is your messaging. Even if you supply them with informative, cutting-edge sales and marketing collateral materials, you cannot control how they present your company or your products to the potential customers. You cannot control how they advertise your products or services, unless the advertising is part of a cooperative plan that is closely administered by your marketing department. You probably have other partners who represent your company and your message. They might be vendor companies that market complementary products and sometimes bundle your products or services with their own products. What control can you exercise over these partners and how can you ensure message consistency? You certainly can't oversee joint marketing if your company doesn't get directly involved in monitoring and contributing to message content. Part of the solution is being involved in message and script creation. The other part of this solution occurs in the initial selection of partners.

Any time there are other companies marketing and selling your products, the chances of inconsistent or inaccurate messages being broadcast by their sales or marketing people increase significantly. You cannot stand over every salesperson and correct inaccuracies as they occur during the sales process. Your best bet is to determine the exact level of knowledge they will need to meet both your company's and the customer's expectations, and see that they get that information in the form of training and sales collateral materials. Your training curriculum and sales literature should be reviewed and updated frequently. To ensure that the messages being broadcast by your partners match your own product messages, you will have to send your own people out and let them spend time in the trenches with your distributors, resellers, and other partners so that you can monitor the content of their pitch and provide them with feedback on the accuracy of their messaging. Consistency in messaging is what marketing alignment is all about.

Why is this so important? First of all, if the messages emanating from your company or your partner companies are mixed or inconsistent, it will create market confusion. Potential customers are more likely to postpone or even cancel plans to purchase your company's products if they perceive inconsistencies or a lack of clarity in your articulation of your product's benefits or positioning. Consistency is a key factor in addressing this issue. The other key has to do with matching customer, market, and influencer expectations. If the influencers pronounce that benefit X is the most important benefit to customers in your targeted market segment and the customers agree, then your message better emphasize that benefit. And your product had better have a substantial competitive advantage over other products claiming to have benefit X. If your company ignores customer, influencer, or market expectations and declares your advantage to be benefit Y, then you will not succeed in this market space.

Inconsistency comes when one department or area of your company is broadcasting message A while another department is broadcasting message B. Marketing might be promoting benefit X, while your sales group is telling customers that the most important benefit of your offering is Y. And your sales channel partners could be articulating Z as the primary advantage of your company's offering. Doubt and uncertainty will destroy a company's ability to build credibility and momentum in any market space. A coordinated effort will reap significantly more revenue and market share than a disjointed effort. You cannot expect to achieve

## Chapter Two: The Elements of Marketing Alignment 41

market leadership unless your positioning and value proposition are both on target. Every message being communicated by your sales and marketing groups has to be on target. Your partner's messages have to be on target. And they all have to be in harmony with customer, influencer, and market expectations. If your messaging does not meet these criteria, then the problem could escalate and conceivably cost you your company in the long run.

So how does this happen? It's the result of poor communication inside and outside the company. The biggest contributor to this dilemma is the lack of communication between individuals, departments, and divisions. Add a dose of management apathy and the cycle is complete. Companies have a habit of bureaucratizing once market momentum is established. As departments or divisions grow in size and number, they have a habit of moving towards independence. Management tends to promote vertical communication, as in up and down the organizational chart, while their horizontal view corridors collapse. This translates into horizontal or departmental myopia and can have a catastrophic impact on any organization. Sure, it's important to maintain vertical communication within the chain of command, but internal information sharing has to move sideways within the company, from department to department and division to division. Internal information sharing should not only be encouraged, but facilitated at all levels by management

A lot of companies and corporations squander some of their more valuable assets, like internal intelligence, because they have yet to develop proper communication systems. For example, if the company's product development group does not have access to the knowledge base in the customer service group, then they have no clue about their customer's needs, expectations, and requirements. How would they know what product enhancements current customers would expect to see included in the next version of the product? How would they know if there were a myriad of complaints concerning a specific product function? It might very well be easy to update the product and address these problems. If customer service does not have the opportunity to share their knowledge with marketing, product development, or sales, how will any of these groups know about these issues, let alone be able to address them?

The customer service group has a wealth of knowledge that should be shared with a number of different departments. There are numerous opportunities for communication breakdown to occur within the company, especially if management does not act proactively to ensure that this type of intra-departmental information exchange is encouraged and enforced.

Here's an example. The corporate sales group has recently become aware of the fact that many of their targeted clients have eliminated their company's product from consideration because they believe that the company's product is missing specific functionality or features. The product actually does have this functionality and these features. Maybe these specific features were not emphasized in the product literature or advertising, or maybe they were completely left out of the marketing materials. How valuable would it be for the company's marketing group to have this information? If there is no marketing alignment coordinator to facilitate this internal knowledge sharing, then management should appoint someone to this role and make that person accountable for this information flow. Internal communication is the key. This is the oil that will lubricate the organization and keep it running smoothly and efficiently. Market leaders have systems in place to facilitate this type of intra-departmental communication and information sharing.

## *Targeting*

Targeting is not just about markets, market segments, or customer types. Companies have to include partners and influencers when determining their targets in the battle for mind share and market share. Alignment has to involve everything a company does in preparing for the marketing wars. If an organization intends to achieve market leadership, alignment should impact every aspect of the organization's fabric. Targeting is an integral part of this alignment process. Traditional marketing types believe that targeting is only about markets and customers. Marketing Alignment requires not only aligning marketing efforts with market and customer segment targets, but ensuring alignment with marketing partners and market influencers as well. Partner targeting is about determining the entities that will be a part of the marketing efforts but aren't necessarily a part of the internal organization or company. Consideration must be given to selection criteria, operational philosophy, and your company's go-to-market strategies and tactics. If your partner's efforts are not

Chapter Two: The Elements of Marketing Alignment    43

in complete harmony with your own efforts, then you are wasting marketing resources and sacrificing your company's market leadership potential.

## Targeting Partners

There are a variety of partner types that will be included in this discussion of partner targeting. Partners can include, but not be limited to, sales channel partners such as dealers, distributors, resellers, mass merchants, value-added resellers, consultants, product integrators, fulfillment houses, and telemarketers. There are other partners involved in articulating your product messages, such as direct onsite service and support partners, and telephone product service and support providers. Your investors are partners and have to be aligned with your vision and goals. If your product does not offer a complete solution, then vendors of complementary products that also contribute to the overall solution would be partners that are not only very important, but strategic to your success. Given the popularity of outsourcing, there are a number of other types of business partners, including suppliers, assemblers, packaging companies, rework facilities, and shippers that assist companies in getting products to market, but are not necessarily involved in your company's marketing efforts. For the purpose of marketing alignment strategies, only those partners that participate directly in your messaging, positioning, and other marketing efforts will be addressed in this section.

Partners most directly involved in your marketing effort are typically your sales partners. Why should choosing your sales partners be difficult or require a selection process? Dealers and resellers are dealers and resellers, right? The more you can bring on board, the larger your distribution system will become and the ultimate result will be more sales and revenue, right? Wrong! For example, if your products require a lot of technical expertise and support, and you try to sell them through mass merchandisers, such as Wal-Mart or Target, you're asking for unhappy customers and a bad reputation. On the other hand, if you sell consumer items that require high volumes of sales to be profitable, but require little or no technical sales expertise, you need high-volume mass merchandisers in your distribution chain. You would not want to sell them through boutique or value-added resellers, whose value lies in providing additional services or technical expertise, but are not capable of high sales volumes. If you did that, you would be shooting yourself and your company in the foot because your company's sales objectives would not be realized. Certainly, these are simplistic explanations. Generally, a lot more thought must be given to your channel partner selection. First, we'll discuss channel structure and its importance in partner selection.

As mentioned in the section on sales channel strategies, sales channel structures are generally associated with product types and product requirements. If your product is a consumer product that is very straightforward in usage and inexpensive in price, it will most likely be sold in retail outlets that generate high sales volumes. The channel structure can be two-tier or three-tier. A two-tier channel structure is made up of the product manufacturer (or vendor) and a reseller. A three-tier channel structure involves a middleman such as a distributor or wholesaler. In the past, most consumer product companies used the three-tier channel structure, preferring not to deal directly with the resellers or dealers. Distributors provide additional services to the resellers that include terms, financing, service, support, warranty coverage, fulfillment, etc. These middlemen eliminate the need for the manufacturers to process and ship hundreds of small product orders. They also take care of all of the billing. However, sales channel strategies have changed with the emergence of vendor direct selling and Internet resellers. The success of national mass merchandisers such as Wal-Mart, OfficeMax, and Home Depot have also had an impact on sales channel strategies. Today, a lot of product manufacturers are entering into direct contracts with mass merchandisers and Internet resellers. Thus, the middlemen, the wholesalers and distributors, are becoming a vanishing breed.

If you invent the ultimate home or consumer product, don't expect Internet resellers and mass merchants to line up at your door. It doesn't work that way. Significant national or international demand for your product will have to be established before any of these companies will consider courting your company or taking on your products. Major resellers and merchandisers typically carry only products that are market-driven. Market-driven products are products for which the demand has already been created, either through major marketing campaigns or grass roots popularity. They are products that enjoy significant popularity within the markets for which they have been targeted. Customers ask for these products by name. In other words, these products are very well branded and have built-in demand. The ultimate in branding is when your product's name is used instead of the product category. For example, a lot

## Chapter Two: The Elements of Marketing Alignment 45

of people will ask for a Kleenex, instead of a tissue, or a Coke instead of a soft drink. This is the pinnacle of branding.

Products come in all sizes, types, and price ranges, as do channel partners. You won't be going to Wal-Mart to buy your BMW. At least, not yet. If you are Ford Motor Company, and you are looking for an enterprise software application to increase your manufacturing division's efficiencies, you'll not be going to the mom and pop computer store down the street to spend your allotted budget—roughly several hundred thousand dollars. Consequently, an enterprise software vendor will most likely use a combination of direct sales executives and global consulting firms to fulfill their sales channel strategy and make that pitch to Ford. And BMW will continue to use their dealer network to sell and service their cars. BMW does not sell their cars through mass merchandisers because those outlets cannot provide the services and support required by BMW. Also, there is a certain amount of exclusivity and prestige associated with BMW dealers that is not associated with mass merchandisers. Given the success of Internet car buying services and their move toward affiliating themselves with some of the national merchandisers, that could change at some point in the future. However, when that happens, it will most likely not involve luxury or prestigious automobile brands. The bottom line is that your sales channel has to be in alignment with your product's pricing, target market, and technical, service, and support requirements.

Product vendors have to make sales channel partner selections based on similarity of approach, philosophy, and market targets. Companies have to ensure that their channel partners are using the same messaging and value propositions in marketing these products. A mixed product message is the wrong message and can destroy a product's sales and market leadership potential. In order to become a market leader, your channel partner should be a market leader or have the potential to be a leader in the markets they service. Channel partners that move a lot of your competitor's products are not necessarily bad selections. However, if they sell an abnormally large percentage of your competitor's products, they're probably overly biased towards those products and will not do a good job with your product line. An abnormal percentage is a percentage far above the competitor's national market share average. For example, if your competitor has 35% share nationally, and one of your targeted channel partners has raised that share to 50% in their market area, they would not necessarily be a good partner. On the other hand, if you are sure they're convinced that you have a better product than your competitor, they might be able to achieve the same results for your product. Healthy competition is great as long as your product provides superior differentiation, and your resellers understand and can articulate this differentiation. You cannot control what your resellers say about your products; however, if you provide them with above-average training, sales materials, and incentives, hopefully they will articulate your product's advantages in an accurate and compelling manner. That should give you the success you are looking for in terms of revenue and market share.

There is another sales channel partner type known as a rep firm. Rep firms can act as wholesalers who sell to the resellers, or they can sell direct to the targeted customers. Typically, rep firms represent the vendor as their primary sales force. They don't stock products, fulfill orders, finance, or provide any other services associated with distributors. They are simply an outsourced or contract sales force. In most cases, rep firm sales people are easier to mold, shape, and train. Just remember that your product will most likely not be the only product your rep firms or your other channel partners will be offering. They might not place the emphasis on your product that you're expecting. It is up to you to do an in-depth investigation on the front end to learn everything you can about how these potential partners work with other vendors and how successful they are in moving products and maintaining a satisfied customer base. Distribution partners, resellers, dealers, consultants, and rep firm salespersons all represent your company and your products to their target customers. Choosing the best possible sales channel partners is critical, regardless of what type of channel structure is employed. For those companies who exclusively use channel partners or third-party outside sales teams, it is especially critical. Conversely, those companies that use their own sales representatives should not encounter these issues and should have minimal problems with regard to approach and presentation.

Sales channel partner selection should be done with a great deal of research, investigation, and face-to-face communications. During this process you can ensure that expectations are set on the front-end, and there are no surprises. Channel structure must be considered thoughtfully in the selection process. How a partner integrates into the proposed structure is a fundamental consideration. There are those who believe that a company cannot have too many resellers, regardless of their fit and integration into the vendor's proposed channel organization. Alignment is critical here for both initial revenue generation and future market leadership. If your channel partners are not leaders in their markets or at least rising stars, how can you expect to become a leader in your market?

In analyzing prospective channel partners, keep in mind that they should be judged the same as a prospective employee of the organization. Do they fit in with your company's mission, its values, and marketing philosophy? The best indicator of the channel partner's potential will be their previous successes in your target markets, and their reputation within that market space. A partner with a questionable reputation will soil your company's reputation. Sales success in your market does not compensate for a bad reputation or image. It would take an enormous amount of damage control to overcome such a stigma. There are those less-than-savory marketers who move a lot of product, but do so at the expense of the customers and their overall satisfaction. Head it off at the pass, nip it in the bud, or do whatever is necessary to ensure it doesn't happen. This is not a win/win scenario, so be prudent in your selection process. Remember, you are in this business for the long term. Market leadership requires staying power, and a solid reputation with your customer base.

Besides sales channel partners, there is another type of partner that might be part of your marketing effort. Some products are stand-alone; they are the whole or total solution to the projected customer's dilemma. There are other types of products that are of little or no use without an additional product or products to complete the solution or offering. For example, would you buy a motorboat that did not include the motor? Of course not, unless you just happened to have the necessary motor sitting at home to put in that boat. In most instances, one company manufacturers the boat and another manufactures the motor. The boat company will have to find a partner or partners who can supply the motors for their various lines of powerboats. In some cases, the boat company will market the whole package under their brand; in other instances, the boat and motor will be co-branded. Take market leader MasterCraft. They teamed with GM for their Vortec and Cadillac Northstar engines to provide the power for their award-winning line of ski boats, wakeboard boats, and luxury performance runabouts. The Vortec engines are used in the ski and wakeboard boats, while the Cadillac Northstar engines are used in their luxury performance runabouts. The alignment is definitely there in their association with high-end quality, power, and performance.

Co-branding typically involves joint and individual marketing efforts in which both product companies participate. Even when the boat is marketed under a single brand, it's still important that the motor company does some marketing and it is in concert with the boat company's messaging and value proposition. In the co-branding scenario, the partnership will leverage both brands in their marketing activities, and employ a unified marketing effort that combines their value propositions and messaging. If the boat manufacturer boasts of being the most economical brand of ski boats, and the boat motor company boasts of being the best motor that money can buy, then they are sending conflicting messages and value propositions. This is not the case with MasterCraft. Both MasterCraft and Cadillac are definitely high-end product companies and match up very well in this regard. Their value propositions relate to quality and performance. Both companies target the market segments with corresponding demographics and use similar messages to create a compelling must-buy attitude in the mind of their targeted customer. Companies don't always consider the importance of selecting strategic partners based on their value propositions and their target markets, which can be a very costly mistake. Again, if you expect your product to become a market leader, you'd better select a market leading vendor partner, or at least one who has the same objective and goals and is capable of achieving them.

The partner selection process is part of your go-to-market strategy. It should not be an afterthought, but should be entered into with the same strategic thinking, extensive research, analysis, and consideration as the development of the value proposition for your company and your products. Your channel partners, sales partners, and product partners are as strategic to your success as the viability of your product's success within that market construct. A solid product offering and marketing effort is only as effective as the team that takes it to the market. Select only the best, most appropriate players for your team and the rewards of your diligence will pay off in reduced costs, and increased market share and revenue production.

## Targeting Influencers

Targeting influencers is another area where companies do not make the most prudent or informed decisions. Influencers include journalists, analysts, and the thought leaders in your market space. Since company

## Chapter Two: The Elements of Marketing Alignment         49

executives are not necessarily in the PR or AR loops, their knowledge of which specific influencers significantly impact their markets is generally limited. In some circles, executives believe that journalists that report on their markets are pseudo-intellectuals who couldn't make it in the business world and go out of their way to write unfavorable things about the company's products. There is also a common belief that the best way to achieve favorable press from a particular magazine or journal is to buy advertising space in that periodical. This is generally not true, particularly in the more respected magazines, trade publications, and newspapers. In some cases, the larger advertisers find it easier to have an audience with an editor and tell their side of the story, but that does not necessarily translate into favorable reporting on the company's products or reputation.

The journalists in some industries do have a tremendous amount of influence and can, in some cases, determine the level of success the company and its products will achieve. There are numerous cases in the computer industry. For example, a *PC Magazine* "Editor's Choice" award for a personal computer will translate into millions or even hundreds of millions of dollars of revenue for that computer and its company. Software development companies have based their product development release cycles to coincide with magazine review cycles to ensure that their newest product will be released just in time for the magazine's product review in any given year. The *Motor Trend* "Car of the Year" award can have a similar impact of the success of an automobile. So, indeed, the press can have a tremendous impact on the success of specific types of products. And given the fact that most companies have a limited amount of resources to devote to communicating with and courting specific publications and their editors or journalists, it stands to reason that being able to target the most influential ones in your market is critical to the success of your product or products.

Analysts exist in a slightly higher stratosphere and typically review and report on the larger global industries and markets. In some cases, these markets and industries are more technical in nature as well. Analysts cover industries and high-end markets such as financial services, computer hardware and software, communications, insurance, healthcare, manufacturing systems, pharmaceuticals, automobile companies, defense markets, aerospace, etc. The closest thing to analysts for consumer products is probably the consumer watchdog editors and journalists; the ones employed by *Consumer's Union* and *Consumer's Digest*. Some might consider these analysts, writers, and reviewers as journalists. There is certainly a fine line between the two. In fact, if an analyst does not work for an analyst firm, then it might be said that he is not truly an analyst, although there are many analysts working for investment and brokerage firms.

Analysts have a reputation for being prima donnas and exceedingly hard to access. Analysts are not that different from journalists except they are typically better paid for the work they do and in some instances, more experienced and knowledgeable with regard to the markets and industries they cover. Part of the prima donna image comes from the fact that they have a tremendous amount of pressure placed on their shoulders with respect to workload and time management. They are expected to read reams of information and data, travel across the country constantly, do copious amounts of research, write numerous reports, reviews, and analysis, return thousands of telephone calls and e-mails, and be available to talk to important clients at a moment's notice. You would probably be just as surly if you were put in a similar position. These men and women are human, and can be approached if you understand or take the time to learn the process. There is a definite methodology to initiating and developing relationships with the analysts. This will be discussed in more detail in the alignment process section.

Thought leaders can be either analysts or journalists, a combination of both, or none of the above. Thought leaders are those folks whose opinions are highly respected and sought after in a particular industry or market space. Their opinions and commentary are viewed as the gospel in that particular industry segment, product area, or market. Thought leaders are best-selling authors who have written one or more books about a particular market, industry, or product area. In other instances, they have founded and/or managed market-leading companies in a particular market or industry segment. They provide their opinions on major market events, product introductions, or other phenomena that take place in an industry.

Lee Iacocca of Chrysler fame is an example of a thought leader, both in the automobile industry and management philosophy sector. Louis Gerstner, IBM's illustrious CEO and the man responsible for IBM's recent turnaround, would certainly be considered a thought leader and visionary in the areas of corporate management, technology marketing, and corporate turnarounds. Jack Nicklaus is considered a thought leader

## Chapter Two: The Elements of Marketing Alignment 51

in the golf industry in both course architecture and equipment development. When one of these folks endorses a product, a business concept, or a management philosophy, it has a very positive and significant impact on the success of the product, concept, or philosophy. Accordingly, if you are marketing basketball shoes and Michael Jordan endorses them, chances are you will be successful. Just ask Nike. Or if you've just introduced a time and life management scheduler and Steven Covey, the author of the *Seven Habits of Highly Successful People*, endorsed it, you could be pretty confident that it would be successful.

Regardless of whether the influencers in your market space are journalists, analysts, or thought leaders, or a combination of all three, they will play a very important role in both the success of your company and its products. Influencers can and do help shape the expectations of your potential customers and clients. It is imperative that they are on your side. You cannot simply suppose that they will see the benefits of your offerings or products. You must communicate your message and value proposition to them in a way that they can connect with, and whatever you do, do not make them feel as if they are just another target of your company's marketing pitch. In fact, the last thing you will want to do is to communicate with them in the same way you would communicate with a potential customer. Pardon the bluntness, but they are not at all interested in your marketing B.S. They are, however, interested in facts, figures, accurate product claims and product comparisons, along with supporting evidence in the form of case studies, white papers where appropriate, and success stories. Their time is very limited and they would prefer that you cut directly to the chase. They want to know what your product does, how it is different, why it is better, and what your value proposition is all about. And then they want to see proof to back up what you say. Influencers tend to take the same tack as actor/director Jack Webb, from the old television series, *Dragnet*. They require only one thing from you, and that one thing is "...just the facts, only the facts..." about your offering. So make it easy on them and give them what they want. It will go a long way towards establishing credibility and providing a foundation for a solid relationship.

Why would you think it is so important to identify the top five or ten influencers in your market space? I'm sure that your company does not have an unlimited press/analyst relations budget or the personnel to go after every journalist, analyst, and thought leader in your market space.

Can you afford to seek out every influencer in your market? Not no, but heck no! If your company is large, you can target more influencers, but doesn't it make more sense to identify the primary influencers in your market space and apply all of your resources to them? This has to be preferable to taking a shotgun approach and hoping that you can connect with the most influential journalists, analysts, and thought leaders. It really does make more sense to concentrate on the top five or ten influencers, and do a better job with them in establishing credibility and building relationships. Resource management is critical to optimizing this effort, and ensuring your ultimate success in the market. In most markets, if you cannot convince the influencers, you will have no chance of convincing your potential customers or strategic partners. You want to win this game, right? Well then, use your head. In those markets, you will have to win at this game to survive. With the right approach and the correct strategy, the influencers will become an integral component of your marketing effort and you will win.

## Targeting Customer and Market Segments

Customer targeting begins with your value proposition. Companies do not go into business thinking there is a particular customer segment that they want to target and then look for a product that will appeal to that target customer. Invariably, a company is built around a product. Generally, there is an unfulfilled need that this product addresses. It addresses this need better than any other products or offerings in the market. Even if the company management is quite sure that they know exactly which specific customers will benefit from this product or service, it is still important that the value proposition be validated. Another critical element to this process is an extensive review and analysis of the competitors in the targeted market segment.

The value proposition matrix (as shown in *Figure 3*) was discussed in an earlier section of this book, but we will revisit it to ensure clarity and its relative importance in the alignment process. Development of the value proposition begins with construction of a two-dimensional matrix listing product applications (uses) on one axis and potential customer/user segments on the other axis. This exercise should be undertaken by a group of individuals that have a good understanding of the product concept and a stake in the success of the product. Typically, this would be the core

## Chapter Two: The Elements of Marketing Alignment 53

group of initial employees and/or senior management, depending on the maturity of the organization. If the company is a startup, then there will be only a few employees and the entire staff should be included in this exercise. If the company is established and this is just a new addition to the product line, then the value proposition team should include individuals from engineering, development, marketing, sales, product management, finance, manufacturing, and senior management. If the product falls into the same channel distribution already in place for the company's other products, a few selected channel partners should also be included in the team.

Once the team is assembled, the process begins with construction of the matrix. The more input the better. Creative thinking is usually most effective when several points of view are represented among the team members. This results in a more comprehensive development of the value proposition matrix. Numerous scenarios should be offered up and given thoughtful consideration when filling out the matrix. This is not a fifteen-minute exercise. A few hours should be expended to come up with all of the possible combinations of customer/application sets. Each possible combination should be thoroughly and thoughtfully discussed, analyzed, and evaluated for inclusion in the final list. After your team has compiled a reasonable number of plausible iterations and combinations, the matrix should be finalized. Once complete, the matrix document should be distributed to each member of the team. Each member will then attach a weighted score to every combination in the matrix. Given the size of the company, and the experience and background of the employees, a larger group of employees could be used for this matrix evaluation. The team leader can determine who should be involved in the user/application plausibility selection. Once the team has weighted the matrix value propositions and the results are tabulated, select the top three or four user/application scenarios receiving the highest weighted averages. Now, you're ready for the next stage of the process.

The next stage in the process involves researching competitive products and offerings to ascertain if you can successfully differentiate your product's value proposition from the market leaders' value propositions. Remember, *successful differentiation involves being able to make an undisputable claim about your product that your competition cannot make, and one that will create a must-buy attitude in the mind of the targeted customer segment.* It should be noted that if your claim is not specific, but general with regard to competitive advantage, it will have no merit and no real advantage. If you just say that your product is faster or better, but you cannot provide tangible proof, then you have no differentiation or competitive advantage. On the other hand, if you can demonstrate a feature or features offered by your product that your competitors cannot match, then you have tangible proof of your product's superiority. A product's differentiation has to offer a very compelling reason for purchasing that product or there is no real advantage.

It is also very important that you understand that regardless of whether or not you can successfully differentiate your product in the market place, if your competitor is the market leader with a lion's share of the market and unlimited marketing resources, you still may have a very difficult time penetrating the market. The competition could quite possibly revamp their product to match yours and do this in less time than you believe possible. There have been instances where market leaders simply change their advertising copy to include claims similar to new market entrants. Even when these claims are not truly accurate, they can take the wind out of your sails and you lose. Is this ethical or responsible? No, but it's more common than you might suspect. And if it works, they probably won't lose much sleep over it. If there is a dominant market leader in your target market with virtually unlimited resources, it might be advisable for you to reevaluate your go-to-market strategy and target a narrower market segment. With fewer resources, it sometimes makes more sense to target a smaller, better-defined customer segment that maybe the dominant market leader has been ignoring. It will take more research and market validation to make these determinations. However, if the customers in that segment truly feel neglected and you revise your offering to be more appealing to them, your hard work will pay off and you will be on your way.

Once your value propositions have been constructed and narrowed down to three or four, it's time to validate them. First, however, do the research and determine the size of the specific market relevant to each value proposition. The largest markets will also be the ones with the most serious competition, but if your differentiation is considerable, your entry into the larger market could provide a much larger return. If the market leader is solidly entrenched in this market, it might be difficult to successfully enter this market even with a highly differentiated offering. Also, investigate and determine if entry into a smaller, narrower market segment will allow expansion into the larger market once you have succeeded in the smaller market segment. These considerations are essential in determining the market you will ultimately pursue. The amount of go-to-market resources available to you will be a primary factor in deciding which market to enter. Take one step at a time. Remember, first things first. Validate each individual value proposition. To do this you will have to survey potential customers in each market segment to determine which value proposition has the best chance of success.

The next three paragraphs elaborate on the value proposition validation *survey* process, which was discussed earlier in this chapter. Skip these paragraphs if you feel confident that you understand the survey development, implementation, and tabulation process. Validating your value proposition is the most critical component of your go-to-market strategy. Achieving market leadership is not possible if you muck it up.

The survey can either be accomplished via the telephone, the Internet, direct mail, or in person through a focus group. Direct mail and the Internet are generally the least expensive methods to employ. Regardless of the medium used, a questionnaire will have to be created. The questionnaire will include questions that relate to the potential customer's buying habits, decision-making elements and process, sales channel preferences, product information sources, influencers, and other pertinent requirements of the product. It is best to limit the questionnaire to twenty objective questions or less. The final question in the survey should ask the respondent if he or she would buy this product based on a short one-paragraph description of the product including its value proposition. A survey should be done for each customer segment and its related application.

A gift, premium, or incentive will ensure a much higher response rate. Do not expect respondents to complete the survey out of the goodness of their hearts. It won't happen. Surveys with no incentive will return maybe a 2% response rate, while those with premiums have been known to return as high as 50% percent. You should not spend less than three dollars or more than twenty dollars for these incentive gifts. Make sure that the questionnaire is easy to tabulate. Multiple choice and true false questions are the best choice for easy tabulation. You can include one or two subjective, essay-style questions if there is some information that can only be obtained through asking such questions. Avoid them if you can, but sometimes there is no feasible alternative. Example: "What features would you like to see included in this type of product that don't exist in any other products offered for this application/purpose?" In fact, if you ask such questions, be sure to put some limit on the answer like features a, b, c, and d. Also, make the respondent rank in order their answers to such questions. That way you can determine which features or problems are most relevant to your offering. If it is truly an essay question, provide four response lines. Once the surveys have been completed, what do you do next?

Tabulate the responses on your surveys and measure the results. For instance, of the four questionnaires, the responses indicate that there was only one value proposition where the potential customers overwhelmingly said they would buy your product. An overwhelming response would fall in the 60-90% range. If you believe you have the necessary resources to compete in this market with the market leading competitors, then go for it. If not, maybe it's time for another round of fund raising. Once the decision is made to enter a market, the next step is to formulate a sales and marketing plan that aligns with the potential market segment's buying habits, decision making processes, areas of influence, sales channel preferences, and so on. If you want to raise your confidence level, do a second survey and gather more specific data on each step of the customer's buying process.

What if you tabulate the results and discover that only 35% of the potential customers for a given value proposition would be interested in buying the product? Determine if that 35% of the customers will be enough to make your company profitable and provide growth potential for the future. We are not talking about 35% of the total market segment. There's a difference between the size of the total market segment and the number of customers that you can touch with your marketing efforts. What if your surveys tell you that you would not be competitive in any of the markets surveyed? Will you go for it anyway? You bought this book, so hopefully you're smarter than that! How about...it's time to go back to the drawing board and invent a different, better widget.

Let's assume that you've validated one or more of your value propositions. If you have more than one choice, it would be advisable to study the market dynamics, the growth projections for that market, the competition, and the relative ease of entry for each market under evaluation. Remember that a large piece of a small pie is generally preferable to a small piece of a large pie. The reasoning here has to do with the idea that it is easier to compete with companies closer to your own size than those with infinitely more and better resources than your own. And even if you want to enter the larger market, there are sub-segments of that market where you can remain under the radar of the dominant market leaders long enough to get a decent share and significant revenue. Then, when your company reaches a size that will allow it to compete effectively with the big boys on their own turf, you'll be in a much more favorable position to do just that.

Choosing a market to enter is considerably more complicated than just validating your value proposition and understanding the demographics and profiles of prospective customers in your target segment. Yes, you have to do those things first, but then there is a certain amount of market research required in getting your arms around a strategically sound go-to-market strategy. Take this process very seriously! You usually only have one chance to make a big splash in your chosen target market.

## *Market Forces and Emerging Trends*

In your research, don't overlook emerging market trends and other market forces. Read outside the lines. Look for emerging trends and technologies that could change the whole composition of the market you are looking to enter. These disruptive technologies could even displace your offering and make it obsolete before you even enter that market. There are disruptive technologies being researched every day that can begin to alter the natural evolution of a market life cycle in a few months and completely wipe out that market in a few years. Personal computers, CD players and recorders, digital cameras, voicemail, the Internet, cell phones, fuel cell technologies, and lasers are a few examples. When personal computers first arrived on the scene, who would have thought that they would completely replace typewriters? Well, they did. Digital cameras are having a profound impact on film cameras and the photo processing industry. Who would have predicted that five years ago? Consequently, research cannot be confined to only trade publications that relate to your business. Read cutting-edge publications that cover new emerging technologies and developing trends in science and technology. You don't have to subscribe to a large number of magazines and newspapers. Most of them are available on the Internet and provide categories and titles about the content on their individual home pages. These publications, in print or online, will help you keep abreast of the changing faces of progress and technology in the world today. Don't expect your intended market to have a long life span. As your business grows, add lines of complementary products to diversify your product lines and insulate your business from sudden changes in the market place.

There are other market forces that you will have to deal with as well. When product lines reach maturity and are closing in on the end of their life cycle, they can become commoditized. In other cases, they could become bundled with other mainstream products. Commoditized products are products that have effectively reached the end of their product life cycle and have become so common and standardized that price becomes the primary differentiating factor. The only company capable of competing in such a market is the dominant market leader whose brand is synonymous with the product category.

Bundled products tend to lose their value because they become a component of a larger product value proposition. A successful network software and hardware company, Artisoft, Inc., should have seen the writing on the wall back in the early nineties. The company's main product line, low-cost networking software, began having to compete with Microsoft's entrant into this market space, Workgroup for Windows. Microsoft bundled their network software with their Windows Operating System software, which essentially made it free when the customer purchased a PC. Sound familiar? Microsoft's tactics in this area are well documented.

Artisoft's other primary offering was its network interface cards, the hardware component of the networked PC. The dominant market leader in network hardware at the time was 3Com, which was very well branded and had a major share of the market for these cards. The Taiwanese and Korean board manufacturers started manufacturing these cards and selling them for 20-40% of the pricing of Artisoft's and 3Com's products. The network interface boards had become a commodity in the market place. Because of brand equity and the effort of the large corporations to standardize on a particular brand, 3Com managed to weather the storm for a few years. Artisoft, on the other hand, lost significant market share and revenue during the next few years.

If Artisoft had diversified its product lines during the mid-nineties by adding other complementary networking products such as routers, switches, utility software, and the like, it would have been much better equipped to weather the storm of competition in the network markets. I actually made a presentation to the Board of Directors of Artisoft at that time and I told them that the company was like a top fuel Dragster with only a couple of gallons of gas in the tank. We had great brand recognition and an unbelievable sales channel organization—some 23,000 resellers—but we were rapidly running out of products to move through that channel. My speech fell on deaf ears. The company did ultimately add computer telephony products to its mix in the mid-nineties, but since that product line was out of alignment with its sales channel structure, the company did not maintain its momentum and is a much smaller company today than it was during its heyday.

## *Tie it all together and you have marketing alignment!*

Let's review what you've learned up to this point. Your organization has to begin with a mission statement and a strategic positioning statement. You should be able to relate in a couple of sentences what your organization does, how it does it, why it is better than its competitors, and the overall value proposition of the organization. The mission statement will add your company's direction, its vision for the future, and some values that you absolutely have to tell the world. Next comes your product's positioning and value proposition. It's a lot like your company's strategic positioning statement in that it describes what your product does, how it does it, how it is different than your competitor's product, and why it is better—its competitive advantage, and its overall value proposition. Your company's messaging should tie together the company's mission, its corporate positioning, its product's positioning and value proposition. It must be consistent, coherent, and compelling, regardless of whether it is being broadcast by the marketing group, the sales team, or any of your company's strategic partners. Your company and product messaging should also reflect customer, market, and influencer expectations. In fact, even when the press or the analysts are writing or talking about your organization, their message should be in line with the company line. When any message or image about your company or products emerges, it has to align with both your company's and the market's expectations and requirements. That's what marketing alignment is all about.

# CHAPTER THREE

# MARKETING ALIGNMENT AND CORPORATE SUCCESS

*Marketing Alignment and Corporate Survival*

So what does this marketing alignment concept have to do with corporate survival, let alone market leadership? In the past couple of years, the U.S. economy has gone to hell in a hand basket, and the technology sector in particular has fared worse than the general U.S. economy. Companies have been in survival mode for the past couple of years. Yes, the stronger organizations survive and in some cases thrive. The majority has not fared so well. To a large extent, when the bottom dropped out of the Internet business sector in 2001, it caused the downturn in the technology sector. There was a feeding frenzy by the investment community aimed at the Internet startups beginning in the early nineties. Investors temporarily forgot the principals of business and invested heavily in this sector. Sure, the Internet was and still is changing the world, but not to the extent once believed by the prognosticators and investors.

A great many of these companies had no real business plan or hope of sustained revenue growth, but that did not seem to matter to the investors most of the time. For that matter, analysts, journalists, and thought leaders got caught up in the belief that the Internet would, in and of itself, boost the economy to new heights never before achieved. Following the downturn in technology, the U.S. economy went south, and that caused a major tightening of the corporate budgets. This, in turn, brought about less technology spending, which poured gasoline on the fire known as the technology sector downturn. So, whether your company or proposed company is in the technology sector or a more general market sector or industry, you will need to implement a marketing alignment program to insulate your company from the effects of the economic downturn. Marketing alignment is also necessary if you have any visions of achieving market leadership.

In slow economic times, businesses generally cut costs, right? That's all well and good, but isn't it somewhat important to maintain your revenue streams? If the market for your product is shrinking, and you have X% of that market, what will you have to do just to maintain your current revenue stream? Answer: get more market share! And if you're reducing your expenses and downsizing your staff, how can you expect to get more market share and revenue than your company was generating when you had a full complement of staff and a larger budget? You will have to make more effective use of your existing resources, correct? Not exactly rocket science...or is it? Some companies never get it. The trick is to outmaneuver your competition by gaining more market share with fewer resources. How is that possible? You use your company's marketing resources and efforts more effectively. Marketing alignment will help you do just that. Let's take a look at exactly how one goes about achieving more with less, and beating up on the competition.

There is one additional consideration before we get this company wagon back upright and begin heading for Pinnacle Peak. Let us, for a moment, think about the fact that unless we are the lead dog of this sled we call our market, we have a longer, more difficult road to travel in order to survive and thrive than the market leaders. The smaller the company and the fewer the resources, the less chance there is for survival in a down market. If your company is not the dominant market leader, then your struggle will be much tougher and more difficult. Market leaders have the edge. They know that a declining market is the very best time to go after the smaller players and eliminate as much of the competition as possible during this period. They are aware that the little guys have fewer resources and are less likely to use them effectively. So the major players will increase their efforts to put the smaller companies out of business, and their sales and marketing efforts will be in alignment.

Even if they cut their resources, chances are they will eliminate most of the fat from areas other than their marketing and sales. They know that

## Chapter Three: Marketing Alignment and Corporate Success 63

it's much easier to crush the competition during poor economic times. Think about it. If your corporate life depends on gaining more market share to maintain your revenue streams and you have a bunch of angry stockholders breathing down your neck, would you make cuts in the marketing budget before you made cuts in other areas and departments of the corporation? Not likely. They're confident that the best strategy is to kick the little guys while they're lying on the mat and eliminate them for good. And in most instances, the market leaders have ample resources to do just that. So what can the smaller companies do to keep from getting crushed? How about making the most judicious use of the resources at hand? Just because a company isn't a market leader doesn't mean the smaller company can't use the same strategy as the market leader, and even take it one step further with a superior strategy that optimizes its resources and tactical programs. And that is where marketing alignment comes into play.

The three primary objectives of marketing alignment are *increasing revenue, increasing market share,* and *reducing marketing costs as a percentage of revenue.* In other words, do more with less. Just because your organization has fewer resources, that doesn't mean that you can't compete. You do have the advantage of being smaller and more nimble. That means reacting more quickly to changes in the market and outmaneuvering those lumbering giants that cannot change direction as quickly. This is critical to your company's survival and ultimate success. You do want to become a corporate mogul and retire to your private island in the Caymans? Of course you do, and that's what this is all about...success. There is one important assumption that you are making about your business. And it better be a correct assumption if you expect this concept to work. Your company must have a viable corporate and product strategy for this marketing alignment paradigm to work effectively. That means that you have to have a viable product. It also means that your product should be clearly differentiated from each and every one of your competitors' products, including the market leader's product. It means that your company must have a clear vision of how it intends to articulate the product's value proposition, and adequate resources to market that product. And finally, it means you have diligently done your homework in the market research area and you are competing in a market with sustainable growth potential.

Normally, most companies only have a few misaligned elements residing in their overall marketing effort, as in *Figure 4*. It really depends on the specific areas from which the misalignment originates. If the key elements, such as corporate positioning, a product's value proposition or positioning, are out of whack, then we might have to start from square one. However, if your business has been relatively successful and your company has been profitable for a reasonable period of time, chances are that's not the case. If you are a startup then the key elements have to be in place. In the sections of this book to follow, you will learn how to evaluate the alignment of all of your company's marketing elements and how to bring all the elements back into true alignment. Marketing alignment is a synergistic concept. Two elements working in harmony will produce more and better results than two elements working separately. It shouldn't be difficult to understand that as more of the marketing alignment elements move into place and begin working in true harmony; the outcome of this alignment will be a significant increase in revenue production and market share. If you achieve true alignment, revenue and market share growth will increase geometrically.

## *Intra-company Communications and Corporate Survival*

First, let's spend a little time discussing the importance of intra-company communications. It is extremely important to understand the value of bi-directional communications and intra-company information sharing within the organization. We mentioned horizontal communications and departmental myopia earlier in the book. *Listening and sharing information are critical to building a successful company and achieving marketing alignment.* Employees within a company are constantly gaining new information that will benefit other members of the organization, but only *if* that information reaches those individuals, groups, departments, or divisions. It could be customer input concerning a feature or benefit missing from a product. It could be influencer input on how another company is achieving success in the market at the expense of your company. It could be information gleaned from one of your channel partners about selling successes they are experiencing as a result of a new approach. It might be a product defect that is easily addressed by manufacturing if the message is passed on to manufacturing.

Chapter Three: Marketing Alignment and Corporate Success    65

Figure 4
## Degrees of Marketing Misalignment
*One or two misaligned elements translate into minimal misalignment, while major misalignment involves three or more elements out of alignment.*

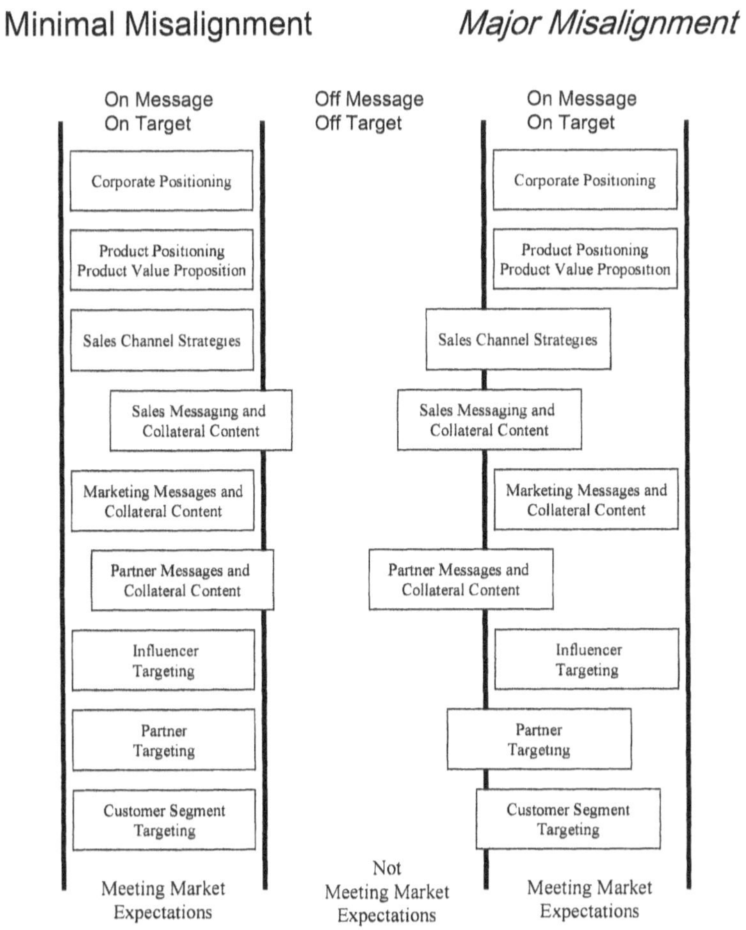

| Minimal Misalignment | | *Major Misalignment* |
|---|---|---|
| On Message / On Target | Off Message / Off Target | On Message / On Target |
| Corporate Positioning | | Corporate Positioning |
| Product Positioning / Product Value Proposition | | Product Positioning / Product Value Proposition |
| Sales Channel Strategies | | Sales Channel Strategies |
| Sales Messaging and Collateral Content | | Sales Messaging and Collateral Content |
| Marketing Messages and Collateral Content | | Marketing Messages and Collateral Content |
| Partner Messages and Collateral Content | | Partner Messages and Collateral Content |
| Influencer Targeting | | Influencer Targeting |
| Partner Targeting | | Partner Targeting |
| Customer Segment Targeting | | Customer Segment Targeting |
| Meeting Market Expectations | Not Meeting Market Expectations | Meeting Market Expectations |

In a number of companies, the communication mainly moves up and down the chain of command as shown in *Figure 5*. If such information is passed along to the right individual in a timely manner, it could mean the difference between creating a market leading company as opposed to mediocre company. *Figure 6* illustrates a better method of communication flow...one that is both bi-directional and horizontal.

### Figure 5
### Hierarchical Communication Flow
*When information sharing only moves up the organizational chain of command and not horizontally – also described as horizontal or departmental myopia*

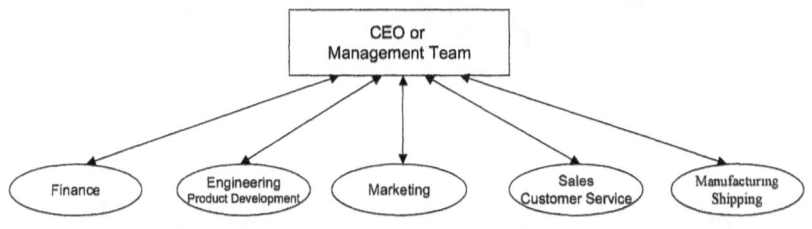

*Information sharing is not effective if department and team members are not communicating directly with each other*

Each and every one of us has been taught how to read, write, speak, and learn. One aspect of our education that is lacking in every level of the educational process is the art of listening. How many classes are offered on listening? Zero. Yet the best way to learn is through active listening. This methodology is central to the marriage counseling process. In order for a relationship to grow and thrive, it is essential that each party learn how not only to listen, but how to understand exactly what their partner is trying to convey. It involves sessions where one partner communicates their feelings to the other, and then the other repeats back to them what they believe that person was saying. This process is considered to be successful when each party reaches a point where they actively listen and understand exactly what the other is saying. This bi-directional communication will then reinforce and strengthen the relationship rather than being a destructive force. The bottom line here is that when the true meaning of the communication is conveyed, the communication is successful, meaningful, and effective.

## Chapter Three: Marketing Alignment and Corporate Success

Why is it that this subject is not part of the curriculum in corporate indoctrination and training classes? Before you can disseminate information within an organization, you have to understand the exact meaning of what has been communicated. And think of the impact active listening has on customer, partner, and influencer relations. All of these relationships are critical to the success of an organization. When it comes to developing your marketing strategy and tactics, the information gleaned from your customers, partners, and market influencers is crucial. Any organization that does not engage and carefully listen to what their customers, partners, and influencers have to say should redirect their business focus and market their psychic expertise. Corporate America would be much more successful if active listening were a mandatory class in every company, and if intra-corporate communications was practiced by every company.

### Figure 6
### Bi-directional, Horizontal Communication Flow
*Information sharing is pervasive within the organization – the most effective method of intra-corporate or intra-company information sharing*

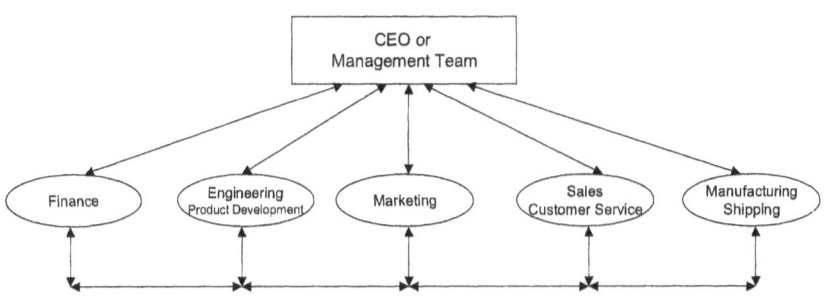

*Information sharing is much more effective if department and team members are communicating directly with each other*

Successful dissemination of internal corporate or company communications is critical to the success of every organization. In really small companies, this should not be a problem, unless the company is made up of socially dysfunctional individuals. However, when the organization reaches a certain size, it becomes very difficult for departmental or divisional employees to get together and share information that is valuable to each group or team. It is conceivable that there are geographical boundaries that preclude this type of communication from ever taking place. Two departments could be on opposite sides of the campus. It some cases, different departments or divisions are located across town or even in different towns. With global corporations, the distance can involve divisions located in different countries.

The point is that if geographic boundaries preclude intra-corporate communications, then the organization will need to implement a system to facilitate information sharing. Typically, a staff member or a team within the marketing group would take on this responsibility and act as the clearinghouse for information dissemination as shown in *Figure 7*. This function is simply too important to the success of the organization to be left up to serendipity. A system must be in place for information sharing to be and effective, positive force within the organization. Okay, I'll step down from my soapbox now. Just remember, you've been informed. Let's get back to examples of the impact of marketing misalignment.

It is easy to see the value of marketing alignment if we look at some typical alignment problems. One of the most common problems has to do with inconsistent messaging coming from different departments within the organization. This is a problem common to almost every corporation or company in one area or another. Let's start with a fictional example. Company A is a power tool company and their marketing group has done its homework and determined that their product's most significant feature in the current market climate is reliability. The influencers have emphasized the importance of reliability as well. The product's current value proposition emphasizes reliability. Company A's customers are primarily contractors who rely on their tools for a living. Their biggest competitor emphasizes low price as their biggest advantage and tells the contractors that their quality is equivalent to company A's products. Company A's sales reps are following their sales manager's advice and pitching the company's reputation for quality instead of reliability. This is a small but important difference in how they are communicating their product's most significant advantage. Their competitors are outselling them simply by emphasizing low price. Company A's marketing team has even provided the sales manager with facts and figures demonstrating the savings that the contractors would enjoy by purchasing a more reliable power tool.

Obviously, if company A's sales reps would talk about value based on reliability, the price argument would not be a significant barrier to selling these tools and beating their competitors. The sales manager has been with company A for many years and in the past could close a lot of sales by touting the company's reputation for quality. Messaging inconsistencies might seem like minor issues, but can have a sizable impact on the company's success.

As companies grow, small power cells typically develop within each department. The department heads sometimes want to control everything in their departments and shun outside input. Communication between departments is either thwarted by department managers, or other circumstances prevent regular communication between departments. In other scenarios, department heads may think they already have the answers, so why would they change the way they've been doing it for years? It might be that departmental proximity precludes regular interaction. Possibly, upper management doesn't think about the importance of facilitating regular meetings between departments. Horizontal or departmental myopia is the phrase coined to describe this situation. If regular meetings took place between the sales group and the marketing group, this important information would be disseminated to the sales group. They would learn about the current customer expectations and requirements and be able to address the customer's needs and sell more products. As mentioned earlier in this chapter, it is critical that an information-sharing system be created, implemented, and monitored to ensure intra-corporate communications effectiveness. *See Figures 5, 6, and 7.*

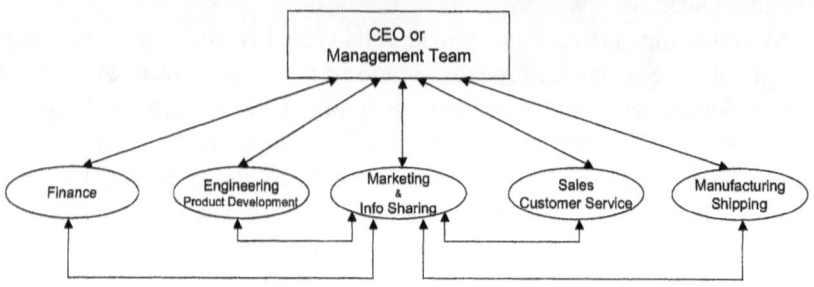

**Figure 7
Marketing as Information Sharing Clearinghouse**
*Information sharing is coordinated by Marketing – the most effective method of intra-corporate or intra-company information sharing in large organizations with significant geographic barriers to effective intra-company communication*

*Information is categorized and prioritized by communications coordinator in Marketing Group and then disseminated to appropriate departments and personnel*

## The Impact of Marketing Alignment on Corporate Success

Marketing misalignment can result when members of the organization do not keep current with changing customer requirements. The marketing group of every company had better keep its finger on the pulse of changing customer requirements or the costs will be overwhelming! Poor alignment or complete misalignment costs companies millions of dollars in lost revenue and reduced market share.

Back in the early seventies, the price of gasoline went up dramatically. For decades, American automobile manufacturers believed they could dictate to their customer base the styling, features, economy, and safety that these prospective car buyers should desire in an automobile. After all, who knew more about what American car buyers should want in an automobile?

High horsepower gas-guzzlers had been the rage for several decades. There was a certain amount of status associated with big V-8 motors. The higher the horsepower, the more status associated with the car. Keep in mind that gasoline was thirty cents a gallon in the sixties. Then the gas prices started to go up and up. GM, Chrysler, and Ford paid no mind and continued to push their inefficient models. About the same time, some new competition arrived on American shores—Toyota, Honda, Subaru,

## Chapter Three: Marketing Alignment and Corporate Success 71

Volkswagen, Datsun (Nissan), Mazda, Fiat, and other foreign marques. Detroit discounted the threat of this new competition and continued selling the cars they believed Americans should and would buy. Unless you've been living under a rock for the past twenty years, you know how this story turned out. The foreign manufacturers have been highly successful in selling their fuel-efficient cars to the American public. Markets are anything but static. If you do not keep up with changing customer needs, requirements, and buying habits, you will enjoy the same fate as the GMs of this world. Lost market share is difficult, if not impossible, to recover.

Marketing alignment problems can undermine your success if you fail to identify the most lucrative target market. Choose the right market and it just might propel your company into a market leadership position. In the early days of the personal computer boom, the most popular software application was a product called VisiCalc. It was the first spreadsheet program for personal computers. VisiCalc enjoyed phenomenal success early on, and helped create the personal computer market. The company targeted individuals, small business owners, and home office workers. Other software developers realized the market potential for personal computers and spreadsheets, and set out to blow VisiCalc out of the water with superior applications that included more features. Programs like SuperCalc from Computer Associates, Context MBA from Context Management Systems, and Multiplan from Microsoft were out to take the market away from VisiCalc. Yes, they offered considerably more functionality, were better programs, and grabbed some market share, but the company that took the market by storm was Lotus Development. Some analysts would argue that Lotus won the market wars by offering an integrated program that included three applications in one program—a spreadsheet program, a database program, and a graphics program. However, SuperCalc and Context MBA also offered integrated application suites with equivalent functionality. In fact, Context MBA offered the three applications that were included in Lotus 1-2-3, along with a fourth application—word processing. So why didn't Context MBA win the spreadsheet wars?

Mitch Kapor, one of the founders of Lotus Development Corporation, decided to bypass the traditional distribution channels for PC applications—computer dealers and retailers. Lotus's sales teams, along with consultants from McKinsey and Co., went directly to the large corporations to sell this new application. The bulk of Lotus advertising went directly into *Time* and *Newsweek* rather than the typical personal computer trade magazines. None of the other spreadsheet vendors realized the impact that corporate America would have on the personal computer and spreadsheet markets. By the way, at that point in time, Microsoft and Computer Associates were the two largest software companies in the world. However, in 1984, both of these giants were blown out of the water by Lotus in the spreadsheet wars. In fact, Lotus exceeded its revenue projections by 1,700% in its first year of operation, and IBM's PC sales tripled in the first three months following the launch of Lotus 1-2-3.

There are a couple of other interesting tidbits about Lotus. Lotus founder Mitch Kapor worked for the software company that developed VisiCalc, which later faded into oblivion. Jim Manzi, one of the McKinsey consultants that helped sell Lotus 1-2-3 to the Fortune 500 companies back then, later became president of Lotus Development Corp. Never underestimate the market potential of a product if it is positioned correctly and targets the most lucrative market or markets available. Solid market research and thorough value proposition validation will go along way in achieving success.

Company survival, consistent growth, and eventual market leadership are the objectives here. Achieving these objectives is even more critical in a shrinking economy. When your market is declining and your company has to increase share to maintain its current revenue streams, marketing alignment is the key to surviving and even thriving. Knowing that the market leaders would like nothing less than to eliminate the smaller companies from their markets should emphasize the need for increasing market share with the same or fewer resources for the smaller companies. It can be done, but it's all about refining and fine-tuning your marketing efforts and then flawlessly executing your marketing plan. If the plan is flawed, i.e. out of alignment, then the execution of that plan is inconsequential to your success. First, get all of your marketing ducks in a row and then you can send them into battle with split-second timing and execution. It is possible for your company to thrive in a down market. A marketing alignment review is the first step in getting a company back on track and moving towards increased revenue production and market share. If there is no one in your company capable of taking on the role of marketing alignment coordinator, then go out and find an outside consultant who can do this job. Just keep in mind that whoever does the job will have to be objective and not mind stepping on some executive or departmental toes in the process. The path to market leadership requires it.

# CHAPTER FOUR

# THE MARKETING ALIGNMENT REVIEW PROCESS

*Internal vs. External Sourcing*

Before the review process begins, a determination of just who will perform the review is in order. In making this determination, it is also important to understand that this person or team will be responsible for the ongoing marketing alignment monitoring responsibilities, or will train the person or persons who will ultimately fulfill this role. In considering this decision, keep in mind that whoever takes on the permanent responsibility will have to step on your executives' toes and point accusing fingers at some or all of your department heads. Consequently, the person or persons fulfilling this role will have to have both the blessing and authority of the CEO. If you put someone in this position that cannot speak and act with authority, then that person will be ineffective in carrying out the mission of the marketing alignment coordinator. So where do we start?

First, let's start with an examination of the internal resources that might be available to perform a marketing alignment review. Is there someone in your organization that has the knowledge, expertise, and time to do a marketing alignment review? Do they fully comprehend everything involved in the process? Are they familiar with your company's direction, positioning, and value proposition? Do they have a product manager's understanding of your product's features, benefits, differentiation, and positioning? Could they develop a product value proposition?

Are they up to date on the competitive landscape in your market space? Could they create a market map for your products? Do they understand the importance of influencers and the definition of a thought leader?

Can this person step away from his or her current responsibilities long enough to perform a thorough evaluation and analysis of your company's current marketing alignment? Can they provide you with a comprehensive report detailing and prioritizing every task that will have to be accomplished in order to bring your sales and marketing efforts into alignment? And can they train someone else to take on the responsibility of monitoring your organization's marketing alignment once they've completed this job and gone back to their original role within the organization?

Finally, consider the return on investment. If you use a high level person from within the organization, how much will it cost you in terms of lost work or inefficiencies due to inattention to their own duties? There will be a return in the form of increased revenue and market share, not to mention, marketing cost reductions. The return on investment calculation with regard to your marketing alignment coordinator selection should be based on the relative cost of using an internal resource as opposed to an external resource.

In most instances, it is probably wise to engage an outside consultant to perform a marketing alignment review. Consultants can bring an objective viewpoint and insights not generally available from within the organization. Insiders may not be able to see the forest for the trees—a sort of internal corporate myopia. In addition, a consultant can be more impartial while working with every department within the organization than one of your employees. Most employees do not have the nerve to correct or talk openly with a high-ranking executive. Consultants are not typically shy when it comes to dealing with executives at any level. Consultants can focus on the job at hand with no outside interference or distractions. Consultants also bring knowledge gleaned from other companies in the form of the best practices and the soundest methodologies learned from prior experience, research or through consulting engagements with past clients. Once you've taken the time to understand what is involved in the marketing alignment review process, making the internal vs. external decision should not be that difficult.

Keep in mind that the person selected will have to have knowledge above and beyond basic sales and marketing. This person will have to

## Chapter Four: The Marketing Alignment Review Process 75

have a good understanding and working knowledge of areas such as market research, influencer ranking, competitive intelligence, emerging market trends, product development, customer service, fulfillment, Web site design, demographic profiling, and more. They will also have to be able to move past the details and tactics and think strategically. Once you have completed this chapter and gained a better perspective on exactly what is involved in the marketing alignment review process, you should be able to determine more precisely the type of person you will need for this job. Then you can make the decision about where to source this individual—from inside the company or from an outside firm.

If the selection is internal, do understand that this is not necessarily a project that can be accomplished by a single individual. The scope of this project has everything to do with the size of your organization and the number of products that your company markets. In a small, single product company, this should not be a daunting task, and could be easily accomplished by a single individual. On the other hand, if your company produces a number of products and sells into several different markets, then this project is much larger in scope. Such a large project will require a team to bring it to successful completion. In this scenario, the CEO or CFO will have to select a team leader and then turn over the responsibility to that person for determining the size and composition of the team. The most effective management technique does not involve micromanaging the project. The most effective management methodology in this case would be to select the team leader, give that person their specific goals and guidelines, and then let him or her select the team and manage the process with no outside interference. The team leader can assign responsibilities and timelines as well as monitor the progress and performance of the team members. Project execution, speed, and quality are enhanced in such an environment. The only time a CEO or CFO should step in is if the project leader meets with interference from one or more high level executives.

If a third party consultant or consulting firm is chosen for the project, there are a number of factors to be considered. In the initial meeting, determine if the consulting firm's representatives listen or preach. If they do most of the talking and don't spend much time asking questions and listening to your responses, that should be red flag number one. If they try to sell you a different set of products or services than what you are requesting, that is red flag number two. If they cannot provide you with a written proposal outlining timelines and costs on the project you are requesting, that is red flag number three. On either of the last two red flags, you have my permission to tell them: "Game over, please leave." Any consultants worth their salt should first try to understand the situation or challenge facing your organization, get their arms around the issues and problems you have outlined, offer their solution, or offer to go back to their offices for the purpose of generating a solution proposal. Be very wary of any consultants that only want to sell you the solution-in-a-box, and cannot offer anything over and above their canned offerings.

A good consultant should be able to provide you with a well-thought-out proposal and a solid business-case for that proposal. They should be able to help you estimate an expected return with regard to increased market share and/or reduced marketing costs. In other words, a good consultant should be able to provide you with the information you need to do the "what ifs" and make a reasonable estimate of the return on the investment your company would achieve in utilizing their services. Rule of Thumb—never hire a consultant unless you can estimate a positive return for the money you spend with that consultant. Duh? I'm sorry, but I had to say it. And by the way, the return should occur in the short term...not the long term.

It is a good idea to estimate the ROIs on using internal vs. external resources. Work up an approximate estimate on the front-end of which approach makes more sense financially. And don't assume that there is no cost involved in using your own people. A lot of very smart people tend to downplay or completely omit the cost of their own employees. Your labor, or your employees' labor, is a valuable commodity. If you take an employee off another task to do something completely outside of their job description, how much does it really cost you and your company? Considerably more than you might imagine. Always factor in the cost of your employees' time along with the lost work they could have accomplished when doing the internal vs. external comparison. You will find that in most cases, it is less costly to source personnel from outside of your company.

## *The Marketing Alignment Review Process*

The marketing alignment review should be a top-down process. Each element of marketing alignment should be reviewed, analyzed, and compared with the others as well as with the customer, influencer, and market expectations. Once the process is complete, then it is time to determine what areas need attention, prioritize them according to importance, assign responsibilities, and associate timelines with completion. One caveat here is that prior to beginning remediation of the individual alignment elements, you will want to get a thirty-thousand-foot view and perspective. It has to do with the "I can't see forest because the trees are in the way" syndrome. If you look at all of your alignment elements as a whole, it becomes clearer how they should fit together and operate in harmony. Then the prioritization process and the timelines required for completion will make more sense. Remember, when you change one piece of the puzzle, the other pieces might not fit together as you had envisioned. Also, the strategic elements including corporate positioning, product positioning, and your product value proposition are all a part of your overall strategy. If you alter or change any of these strategic elements, all of the down-line elements will be affected, and will certainly require some revision, if not a complete overhaul. Sales channel strategies, messaging, and targeting are more tactical in nature. Their structure and content is rooted in the strategic elements. During each step of the process you will need to review, analyze, and compare. Since all of the marketing alignment elements are interrelated, this review-analyze-and-compare methodology will have to be performed as part of the review process for each element, as well as after any changes are made to an existing element. We will walk through the process together.

## *The Corporate Positioning Statement*

The strategy of corporate positioning depends largely on management's view of current and future corporate direction. It also relates to the other companies participating in the same overall market. Your corporate positioning statement should communicate how your company differentiates itself from the other companies competing in your chosen market. It should also communicate how your company intends to assume a leadership position in your chosen market space. Your company could be positioned as the price leader in the market. Your company could aspire to be the customer service leader in the market in which you compete. Your company could be the technology leader by offering the most advanced technology of all the companies in the market. Your company could be the quality leader in your market. Just keep in mind that if you try to say that your company is the leader in technology, customer service, quality, *and* low price, you will have a tough time convincing anyone, especially the market influencers and thought leaders, not to mention your partners and customers. They most likely will not believe that you lead in any of these categories. Your company cannot be all things to all people. Stick with one or two areas where your company and products truly have distinct, measurable advantages, and you will come across as a legitimate contender. Otherwise, they will think you're just blowing smoke up their...well, you know.

Whatever differentiation your company uses in determining its positioning will have to be integrated into each and every product or service value proposition your company offers. It does not make sense to offer one differentiating advantage in one product and another differentiating advantage in another product or product line. If the overriding theme of your corporate positioning relates to quality and value, yet one of the product lines promotes cheap pricing and fewer features than your competitors, your marketing efforts will be out of alignment and you will be sending confusing messages to your influencers and partners. Worse yet, you will be sending a confusing message to potential customers. How costly is that? It would be very costly, indeed. Your corporate positioning is the value proposition umbrella for all of your products and product lines. This does not mean that your products cannot include other advantages that are not included in your corporate positioning...as long as they do not contradict this positioning.

Cisco Systems offers a wide variety of networking and communications hardware and software. They emphasize quality and value. Their products are known for their advanced technology, unmatched compatibility, and high performance. If they offered a product line with questionable compatibility and performance, and promoted these products as the cheapest on the market, would that be in keeping with their corporate positioning? It would not. If Hyundai or Kia, the Korean car manufacturers known for offering some of the lowest-priced economy cars in the American market, introduced a $75,000 luxury car targeted to compete with Mercedes, how do you think the American car buyers would respond to that offering? American upscale car buyers would not react favorably to such an introduction. In both of these examples, such product introduc-

## Chapter Four: The Marketing Alignment Review Process

tions would go against everything these companies represent in their respective markets. It would be like Kmart offering designer suits.

The most important consideration in analyzing your corporate positioning statement is to identify your company's leadership position in its market space and compare it to the positioning of your products. Remember, the corporate positioning statement says "This is what my company does, this is how we do it, this is how we are different, this is why we are better than the other companies that compete in our markets, and this is our value proposition." Corporate positioning is the cornerstone of the structure that is your company. Everything that falls under your corporate positioning should be in line with this statement. That means that every product you sell will have to incorporate the same positioning and a similar value proposition. It is entirely possible that everything from your product positioning and your products' value proposition are in alignment, but the corporate positioning statement does not reflect the products' positioning. It should be easy to fix this, unless the CEO or company founder has a different vision. To fix this, a great deal of diplomacy and compromise would be in order. The main thing is to achieve parity between the company's positioning and the products' positioning, regardless of the approach required. It is also critical that every member of the management team is in total agreement with the corporate positioning statement and a true consensus is reached.

Initiate the alignment review analysis for corporate positioning by answering the following questions:

1. Does the corporate positioning statement reflect the vision and direction of the company?
2. Does the corporate positioning statement clearly differentiate the company from the other competitors in the targeted market space?
3. Does the corporate positioning statement articulate exactly what the company does, how it does this, how it is different from its competitors, why it is better, and the corporate value proposition?
4. Is the corporate positioning statement clear, concise, coherent, and consistent?
5. Does the current corporate value proposition make an undisputable claim that its competitors cannot make, and one that positions the company as a leader within a specific area of the market?

6. Can this statement be communicated in the time it takes to ride an elevator up two or three floors?
7. Is this statement in line with customer, influencer, partner, and market expectations and requirements?
8. Does this statement provide compelling differentiation?
9. Has the statement been updated in the last two years and is it current with regard to the positioning statements of other leading competitors in the market place?
10. Is there a consensus among the management team that this corporate positioning statement is an accurate, clear, and compelling reflection of the company's values, vision, and direction?

Once you have answered each question, you will understand exactly which areas need attention. List and prioritize the areas requiring attention under the Corporate Positioning Section and then move on to the next section. After you complete all of the sections, you can go back and prioritize each section and its associated tasks, and the review process will be done.

## *Product Positioning and the Product Value Proposition*

Product positioning is about your differentiation in the market, and the identification of your competition. Positioning a product in the market is usually the result of exhaustive and extensive research. Generally, a company develops a product that management believes has distinct advantages over the competitors within the chosen market. These advantages will be the core of the product's differentiation. The value proposition associates this differentiation with the potential targeted customers that would benefit most from such a product. The value proposition narrows the target market by identifying the exact customer segments within the overall market. These advantages offer benefits that represent the most important and salient factors considered in the buying decision process by the targeted customer segments. The product positioning statement, like the corporate positioning statement, articulates what the product does, how it does this, how it is different, why it is better than similar products offered by the competition, and the product's value prop-

## Chapter Four: The Marketing Alignment Review Process

osition. As mentioned in the previous section, it is imperative that these claims coincide with the corporate positioning statement.

Evaluate your product positioning statement for clarity, coherence, and the persuasiveness of your product's claim in establishing a must-buy attitude in the mind of the target customer segments. You have to be able to make an undisputable claim about your product that none of your competitors can make. If your competitors have similar advantages, albeit not as distinct as you own, then you should probably return to the drawing board. Your claim has to be undisputable in order to create the must-buy attitude.

And remember, if the market leader in your market space can potentially make a similar claim, regardless of whether or not it is grounded in any factual truth or evidence, you should probably rethink your product strategy. Once a company becomes a market leader, they become believable to the majority of potential customers in that market until proven otherwise. Even then, they can dismiss the detractors as liars or charlatans and, because of their built-in credibility, win the argument in the marketplace.

In some cases, where it is hard to be heard above all the noise in a large market, a company can target a smaller, narrower segment within the larger market and be successful. In such an instance, it is recommended that the offering include additional features that are specific to the requirements of this market niche. For example, a company offering Gore-Tex outerwear wants to market a line of lightweight rain suits. However, there is a dominant player in this field. Perhaps the company might want to add a couple of features that make their outerwear more appropriate for the sailing apparel market. Maybe they could include pockets that accommodate multi-tools or sailing gloves. The company could design the rain suits with more advanced watertight closures for the cuffs and pant legs. Or possibly they could add sailing logos to the outside of the garments. Once the company establishes a solid reputation in this market niche, it could expand its market reach to include hikers or mountain bikers. Prior to entering a market niche, the company would not only have to explore the special requirements of that niche, it would also have to evaluate the market with respect to revenue and growth potential.

Initiate the alignment review analysis for product positioning and the product value proposition by answering the following questions:

1. Is the product positioning in alignment with the corporate positioning?
2. Does the product positioning statement include an undisputable claim that none of your competitors can make, and does it create a must-have attitude in the mind of your current targeted customer segments?
3. Is your product value proposition clear, concise, coherent, and consistent with product and company positioning?
4. Is the target market a viable target for this product and your company based on its size and the competitors within this market space?
5. Based on your product's positioning, would it make more sense to attack a smaller segment of the market, i.e. a niche segment? What product changes would be required to compete in the niche market segment?
6. Has adequate research been completed validating the product value proposition?
7. Has adequate research been completed validating the targeted customer segments for this product value proposition?
8. Is the targeted market segment the most lucrative based on product cost, support and service cost, and the costs associated with selling into this segment?
9. Is there another segment that could provide a better selling ROI?
10. Does the company have the resources to attack this market segment successfully?
11. Do the product's differentiation and advantages correspond with what the influencers believe are most important in this product category?
12. Do the channel partners and/or whole product model partners agree with and endorse your product's value proposition?
13. What is the product lifespan in this market?
14. What are the short- and long-term growth potentials of the targeted market?

Chapter Four: The Marketing Alignment Review Process            83

15. Are there any emerging product, technology, or market trends that would be disruptive to the current market's potential life span?

Once you have answered each question, you will understand exactly which areas need attention. List and prioritize the areas requiring attention under the Product Positioning and Product Value Proposition Section and then move on to the next section. After you complete all of the sections, you can go back and prioritize each section and its associated tasks, and the review process will be completed.

*Sales Channel Strategies*

Now that the product positioning and the product value propositions are in place, the sales channel strategies are next up for review and analysis. Sales channel strategies will be an important factor in ensuring that the product is accurately portrayed in the best light to the most appropriate audience. Your sales channels are the distribution mechanisms that take your product to market. These are the guys that will be articulating your value proposition. These are the guys that will be targeting the market segment or segments that you have chosen. By definition, sales channel strategies are strategic to your success. If poorly conceived, your sales channel strategies could leave your company with channel partners that cannot articulate your product's value accurately. They could also be targeting the wrong customer segments. So making sure that you have reputable sales channel partners who understand your product and can articulate the correct value proposition to the customers that you are targeting is critical to your company's success.

Your product's positioning will dictate the sales organizations that would be your most appropriate sales channel partners. Product positioning identifies your competitors and the market segment you intend to target. Sales channel partners target specific market segments with well-defined product lines. The difficulty does not lie in locating channel partners that sell products like the ones your company offers that target the market segments that your company is targeting. The difficulty lies in finding channel partners that share your vision, values, and direction. The difficulty lies in securing channel partners that will actively campaign and promote your products using the approach and value proposition that you have advocated in your advertising, messaging, and training. Your sales channel strategy should also include the number of partners within specified geographic areas that can achieve your revenue and market share goals.

Other issues involved in reviewing and analyzing your sales channel strategy revolve around your competitors' sales channel strategies. If you set your sales channel strategy based on the approach your competitors were using, you might have taken the wrong approach. When entering a market, choosing the same sales channel partners as the market leaders in your market space might not be the best strategy. Remember the Lotus example. They chose a totally different sales channel strategy from the strategy used by their competitors, and became the dominant market leader in less than one year. If you do use the same channel strategy as your competitors, be vigilant in your partner selection process. Your competitor's channel partners might be the best known and sell the largest volumes of products like yours. However, since they sell products from the market leading companies, they very well may have a bias towards these market leaders and their products. Your sales channel strategy should reflect how involved your sales channel partners are in the customer's buying decision process. If your company produces consumer products and sells them through mass merchandisers, then the sales people have very little influence on the customer's buying decision. In such cases, shelf space location, position, and the amount of shelf space allotted are really more critical to your sales channel strategy and your product's success.

If the sale of your products requires specialized knowledge and a lot of handholding to close the deal, then the choice of channel partners is directly related to your success. It is incumbent on your sales and marketing staff to ensure that your products are top of mind with your channel partner's salespersons, or your products will languish in the stock room. Review the effectiveness of your channel training programs. Do they always have an adequate supply of literature on hand? Have you implemented any incentive programs? These types of programs will go a long way in achieving top of mind with your channel partners. The incentives can be in the form of additional monetary compensation or other gifts for each product sold. Just remember, if your channel strategy does not include any programs for achieving top of mind with the folks that sell your products, you certainly cannot expect to achieve your revenue objectives with those partners. In your review, include an analysis of how the

## Chapter Four: The Marketing Alignment Review Process 85

dominant market leading companies have achieved top of mind with their partners. And do not think for a moment that emulating or copying their methods is unacceptable or a bad idea. If you have a superior product, then you can use their strategies and beat them at their own game.

In your selection process, your channels should have a successful history in selling products similar to your own. These partners should be targeting the customer segments that you are targeting. Certainly it is important to locate the best outlets for selling your products. Your sales channel strategy should include a strategy for ensuring that your sales channel partner locations match the geographic population densities of your customer segments. Your market research should have uncovered this information. It is equally important not to stop there. Do you have the necessary numbers of sales channel outlets to meet your revenue projections? They should have values and sales approaches that mirror your own. They should be established and reliable business partners. You should work together in formulating plans for promotion of your product lines. And you should establish revenue goals and timelines for achieving those goals with each partner. You should have a plan that articulates the overall channel marketing plan, as well as revenue and market share objectives. Competitive and market intelligence gathering have to support your channel strategy and plan. Study your competitors' channel strategies and emulate whichever components of those strategies that you believe would enhance your chances for success.

Initiate the alignment review analysis for sales channel strategies by answering the following questions:

1. Are your sales channel strategies in alignment with your corporate positioning statement?
2. Are your sales channel strategies in alignment with your product positioning and your product value proposition?
3. Are your sales channel partners targeting the identical customer segments that were identified and validated for your product value proposition?
4. Do your sales channel partners employ a sales approach that corresponds with the approach your company advocates?

5. Are your sales channel partners receptive to, and on board with, your product training, sales promotion, and co-op marketing programs?
6. Do your sales channel partners share the same differentiating factors that your company employs?
7. Can you achieve your revenue and market share objectives with your current group of channel partners?
8. Do your sales channel partners share your company's values, vision, and goals?
9. Are there any trends emerging that would make obsolete your current channel structure or operational philosophy?
10. Is there any possibility that your product or products are over-distributed?
11. Is there any possibility that your product or products are under-distributed?
12. Can every one of your sales channel partners provide the level of technical support and customer service required for your products?
13. Are the channels you have selected providing the profit margin and cost of sales you have set in your sales channel strategy?
14. Do your sales channel partners have all the sales tools they need to sell your products?
15. Have you surveyed your channel partners recently to determine if they are receiving adequate levels of product, service, and support from your corporate sales support staff?
16. Do your channel partners cover the geographic regions required to provide your company with the necessary coverage?
17. Do your channel partners provide the revenue and growth potential to meet your company's current and future objectives?

Once you have answered each question, you will understand exactly which areas need attention. List the areas requiring attention under the Sales Channel Strategies section, rank order the issues, and then move on

Chapter Four: The Marketing Alignment Review Process      87

to the next section. After you complete all of the sections, you can go back and prioritize each section and its associated tasks, and the review process will be done.

*Messaging*

Before discussing the messaging review, it would be appropriate to restate the definition of messaging included in Chapter Two. Messaging encompasses virtually all communications emanating from the company's internal departments, along with all of the messages broadcast by external sources such as market influencers, channel partners, and other strategic alliance partners. Even your competitors, your competitors' channel partners, and their other strategic partners messages can impact your reputation and image. Messaging includes messages and presentations originating from every department in your company—from investor relations to management, finance, marketing, marketing communications, press relations, sales, Web content, customer service, and customer support. Channel partners, strategic partners, and third parties such as journalists, analysts and thought leaders also broadcast and communicate messages about your company and its products.

The messaging review should be comprehensive. Review every sentence, every blurb, and every word written, spoken, or broadcast through your advertising, promotion, influencer communications, literature, Web site content, corporate communications, sales communications, image communications, investor relations communications, etc. It all falls under your messaging umbrella. Your reputation, your market status, and your image are all a direct result of your messaging. Everything anyone knows, perceives, or surmises about your company is the result of the combination of messages they have heard or read. Their opinion or viewpoint about your organization has been formed based on the messages they have received concerning your organization. In effect, your company *is* its messaging. Its reputation and position in the market are wholly determined by this messaging. As Geoff Moore stated in his book, *Crossing the Chasm*, positioning is not a verb, but a noun. Your company and its products are positioned by its customers, influencers, and partners. Hopefully, the product positioning you establish will be in alignment with your customers, the influencers, and your partners. Their opinion is the result of the perception they have gained from your messaging.

Messaging is like having multiple artists simultaneously and continually painting a portrait of your company. Any misuse of colors, lines, or textures will muddle the picture. For instance, if the market influencers universally state that the perfect product in your market space is blue, then that is what your messaging should communicate. If your marketing group falls in line with the market prognosticators and broadcasts that your product is blue, you are on the correct track. However, if your sales group is telling customers that your product is light green, the inconsistency will confuse the customers. If your Web site describes your products as purple, you are in big trouble. Consistent and unified messaging that is in alignment with market expectations and requirements is the key. Any messages that are inconsistent, unclear, incoherent, or misspoken will confuse the market. Messaging has to be unified and consistent to be effective. Every message source and every message has to represent your company and products in the very same light. Your messaging comes from so many disparate sources that it provides unlimited opportunities for inconsistency, disharmony, and misalignment. That is why it is absolutely critical to achieve true alignment in your sales and marketing efforts. That is also why you will need some type of centralized content control mechanism.

Traditionally, messaging is supposed to be the exclusive province of the marketing group. So, in essence, an alignment review of your messaging need only confine itself to the content originating from your marketing group, right? After all, they are responsible for advertising, sales collateral literature, press and public relations, channel marketing programs, and any other dissemination of company or product information to the world, right? While in a perfect world that might be true, in reality it is not even close. This review will have to be considerably more comprehensive in scope, and not limit itself to marketing content only.

Remember the early stages of your company's growth? Typically, during the early stages of a company's evolution, marketing does control all of the avenues for information dissemination and commercial communications. As companies grow and mature, it becomes apparent that other internal organizations begin to broadcast their own external company communications. These groups or departments do not intentionally try to create confusion or broadcast misinformation. It just happens. It happens mainly because there is no one responsible for the consistency of the content that is released. The sales group hands out data sheets, brochures, and

## Chapter Four: The Marketing Alignment Review Process

proposals. The customer service group sends out technical bulletins, owner's manual addendums, information on new support programs, etc. The financial department distributes investor relations documents, annual reports, their own press releases, and other notices to shareholders. The Web site passively broadcasts a compilation or distillation of product information, company news, investor information, customer service and support information, upcoming company events, as well as sales information.

So why is it that most companies do not exercise control over messaging? We will examine all of the different avenues for company communications and how the inconsistencies occur. All of the content discussed should be examined in your messaging review. And your marketing department or group is the best place to start. Marketing is the most visible source of messaging in any company. A definition is in order before we continue. A number of people do not understand the difference between sales and marketing. Some people believe these terms are interchangeable. For the purpose of this book, we will define marketing as the entity responsible for developing and maintaining product positioning, and for generating product demand. The tools, materials, and programs marketing utilizes to accomplish this are almost as varied as the companies that make up American business. The sales group is the group responsible for distributing the products to the sales channels, or final customers, in return for payment for these goods or services. Marketing creates the advertising, literature, and other materials that describe, position, and differentiate the product. They also identify and select the mediums through which these materials and/or this information is distributed or broadcast.

The size of the company can impact misinformation dissemination from within the marketing group. Company organizational structures vary widely from company to company, which means that one company might include all marketing functions within its marketing department while another company has separate departments for marketing, marketing communications, product marketing, channel marketing, direct marketing, education marketing, government marketing, Internet marketing, international marketing, etc. If there is a breakdown in the communications between the various marketing departments within the organization, there is a good chance the company will be broadcasting inconsistent messages through some or all of these departments. This is a key factor in performing your messaging alignment review. The size of your company will dictate the size and scope of this review. Some of the messages emanating from these groups will not match the market's expectations or requirements. In fact, even if there is no breakdown in intra-departmental communications, if the group responsible for monitoring the market misinterprets changing or evolving market requirements, they can still get it wrong. In large corporations, the marketing division can be broken down by product lines and have separate product marketing groups for each product line. Even if these groups stay on message, simply creating materials using different styles or formats can cause confusion in their respective markets, or with respect to the company's overall tone and direction.

Here is a hypothetical example. A high-end clothing manufacturer has been positioning their formal wear as the best, highest quality formal attire on the market. The channel marketing group has been charged with moving the current inventory stock as quickly as possible to allow for a new line to be introduced. The channel marketing group puts together a campaign with the tag name "Company XYZ Inventory Stock Reduction Blow-out Sale." This is not really in keeping with the company's image as a market leader in high-priced, stylish formal wear, is it? In fact, the channel marketing group has done significant damage to the reputation and positioning of this company just by choosing the wrong description for this sale announcement. If, on the other hand, the channel marketing group had come up with a more appropriate marketing approach such as "Company XYZ Designer Formal Wear—Uncompromising Style and Quality at an Affordable Price," they would have a much better chance of maintaining their reputation and positioning, and at the same time moving their stock. So even within the confines of the marketing group, inconsistency can rear its ugly head and damage a company's image.

Regardless of the marketing group's organizational structure, it is clear that controls should be in place to avoid inconsistent messaging. If all of the marketing functions are concentrated in one department, the process will be easier. Regardless, after the messaging review is completed, a messaging coordinator should be appointed. This person or team will monitor and approve all company messaging to ensure accuracy, coherence, and alignment. Product marketing, channel marketing, direct marketing, education marketing, government marketing, Internet marketing, international marketing, press relations, analyst relations, and marketing communications will all have to pass any new content along to this messaging coordinator for approval prior to release and distribution. The messaging coordinator will have to be updated on any changes in company or product positioning, differentiation, or targeting by the marketing alignment coordinator or the management team. Naturally, any significant changes in these areas will require a major updating of all messaging content and literature content. In a large corporation, the messaging coordinator will most likely be a full-time position.

Another approach would be to have a designated messaging monitor in each department who meets with the marketing alignment coordinator and the other messaging monitors on a regular basis to discuss issues, problems, and any new directions the company is taking with regard to positioning or differentiation. In smaller organizations, this messaging coordinator position could be assigned to a senior marketing manager or marketing communications manager. In that case, it would be a part of the manager's job description.

## Executive Messaging

Executives in every corporation are required to make presentations covering both corporate and product events and news. The number and frequency of these presentations will depend on the size of the corporation, whether or not it is public, and the industry segment within which the company competes. One thing is certain—unless your company produces super-secret code translators for the C.I.A., your executive team will be on the road giving company or product presentations on a regular basis. And unless your marketing team creates and edits every executive presentation given, there is a very real possibility that the messaging contained within these presentations will include misinformation, inconsistent statements, or wrongly positioned messages.

These presentations typically cover quarterly results and other financial news, corporate reorganization announcements, merger or acquisition news releases, product announcements, investor information, new partner alliances, future growth projections, new product directions, etc. The significance of these presentations to those that follow that company and its market will depend on the leadership position of the company in its respective market and in the overall national or global economy. The importance to the company itself should never be underestimated. If you expect your company to achieve a leadership position in your market space, you had better view each and every executive presentation as very, very important in the overall scheme of things. Achieving market leadership will not happen if you don't take every message broadcast by every member of your organization quite seriously. Your corporate survival depends upon it.

In most instances, your executives will be making presentations that were created in-house, hopefully by members of your marketing team. It is not uncommon for the presentations to be created by the executives themselves or by their administrative assistants. In these situations, see to it that there is a system in place for reviewing these presentations prior to their usage. A messaging or content review person or team should be responsible for reviewing each and every executive presentation. In your initial alignment review, you will have to assign the responsibility to your marketing group and have it review all of the currently used presentations. Its marching orders should be to review each presentation to ensure that it is currently relevant and in alignment with your corporate and product positioning and value propositions. Also, review the presentation for coherency and consistency with all other corporate messaging. Executives sometimes have a penchant for putting their own spin on the message being conveyed in their presentation. This can be the root of the problem. Change one word here and another there, and the original message is diluted or lost. And there are those cases where the executive believes he or she knows better than the marketing group about how the company or product should be positioned or what the value proposition should be. Consensus has to remain intact for an executive team to succeed. Weed out the mavericks if you have no other choice.

When selecting a messaging coordinator from your marketing team, you will have to make sure that the person given this responsibility has the demeanor and authority to revise an executive's presentation and then explain to them why the changes had to be made. This person will have to be immune to the executive intimidation factor. As you can imagine, it will be formidable task for a junior member of the team to tell a senior executive that he is not following the company line and telling the story that needs to be told. If the executive has been schooled in the marketing alignment paradigm and process, that executive should not put up too much of a fight or argue about the changes.

## Chapter Four: The Marketing Alignment Review Process

### Advertising Messaging

The most visible messaging source for most companies is their advertising. Your advertising messages should always be the most accurate statements your company makes with regard to marketing alignment. After all, they should be a direct reflection of your positioning and value proposition. That is, unless you have contracted out your advertising and content creation to an advertising agency, and they have somehow bastardized your message. Even when you use an ad agency to create your advertising message, you should still be able to maintain total control over the content and the message being broadcast in those ads. If you let your ad agency tell you what your positioning and value proposition should be then you're a lemming and you deserve what you get. There are agencies that will gladly take on the entire marketing role, do the required market research, and validate your product's value proposition. In such instances, your advertising message should be in alignment and be the most appropriate message for your particular target market.

If your marketing group creates the advertising, it would be difficult for them to perform an objective review of your advertising messaging. Even if your company uses an ad agency to create the ads and the advertising agency follows the company line with regard to positioning and value propositions, should you still use someone from marketing to review the content? Every member of the marketing team should certainly understand and embrace the importance of messaging and marketing alignment. Given the brevity of the content in most advertising messages, you could use someone from your executive staff not involved in marketing, or someone from your product management or development group to review the messaging. In most cases it doesn't make a great deal of difference who does the review. Just make sure your messaging reviewer asks some leading questions of the marketing team about the creative process and how they arrived at the current positioning and value propositions. Have the reviewer question the validity of the product messaging and value proposition. Marketing should have plenty of ammunition to justify their product positioning and value proposition. Your positioning and value proposition should always be the most prominent and prevailing theme perceived by your target audience from your ads. You can use different approaches in your ads, but the primary message elements should always be the same in every ad. If your advertising is not working, then one of the two ingredients missing. Either your value proposition is no longer valid or your message is not being delivered to the most appropriate audience. Your market research should have provided you with specific information on whom to target and what to tell them. If that's not true, go back and do it again.

## PR Messaging

PR is normally associated with press relations. In some companies, the PR group handles both press relations and public relations. A lot of executives believe that press relations and public relations are the same thing. With the convergence of printed media and electronic media, it hardly seems like there is a difference any more. You call it potato and I call it potatoe...sorry, Vice President Quayle. In this day and time, Media Relations is probably a more accurate description. Press relations and public relations are basically the same thing, although there are a number of announcements that emanate from the PR department that do not target the general public. There are company announcements relating to new sales channel structures, supplier alliances, company reorganizations, management initiatives, etc. that are really of no interest to the general public. Be that as it may, the PR function of every company is an integral part of the company's outgoing messaging system regardless of whom they target with specific announcements and press releases.

In a number of companies, the PR Group is not part of the marketing group. It really depends on the CEO's view of PR's function in that company. Its function is not about product marketing, so why should they be part of the marketing department or division? The PR department's function really has more to do with marketing the company as a whole, and ensuring the company's reputation and stature are kept in high regard by the press and the media. Most companies allow the PR department to wield enormous power over all information that is released to the press about the company's operations and products.

The point here is that the PR department in some companies is given free reign to craft their own press releases and announcements and then distribute these releases and announcements to the specific members of the press and media communities that they have identified. And yes, they do believe that the targeted members of the press and media will use that information in the best interest of the company. That is not always the case. This autonomy given to your PR group can seriously foul up your

## Chapter Four: The Marketing Alignment Review Process

marketing alignment. If the PR group believes it has a better understanding of how the company and the company's products should be positioned and portrayed, then it can make a significant contribution to confusion in your company's market place. Nine times out of ten, the PR group and the marketing group are singing from the same hymnbook and these types of problems do not come into play. However, if you have a renegade PR group who believes it has a better handle on how the company and its products should be described and positioned, you do have a problem.

The most blatant example of misaligned PR that comes to mind was the recent debacle created by Firestone when it was uncovered that the SUV tires they were supplying Ford for the Explorer were prone to delaminate and cause blowouts on those SUVs. Instead of taking the Tylenol approach—assuming total responsibility for the problem and immediately recalling and replacing all of the product, the company announced a staged recall plan and did a lot of finger pointing in Ford's direction. Was that in keeping with a company that promotes quality, durability, reliability, and safety in their value proposition? Hardly. Marketing alignment? They don't need no stinking marketing alignment, do they? *Au contraire*. How many millions of dollars do you think this PR management malady will cost them? How long before Firestone's reputation for quality and integrity is restored? Given, this is not a small mistake, but the small mistakes can and do add up, creating a cloud of confusion that will envelop your company, which is exactly why maintaining alignment with your PR department's messaging is so important.

Some companies have a separate analyst relations group or department, while others delegate this job to their PR group. If your company maintains relations with analyst groups, it will be necessary to include them in your PR/AR messaging review. Companies whose fortunes are determined by the opinion of analysts can ill-afford to broadcast inconsistent messages, or messages not in true alignment with their company and product positioning and value propositions. Companies whose product success is based on analyst reviews should incorporate analyst feedback into their positioning and value propositions. Once they have done this, they can reinforce their status with the analysts by broadcasting messages that reflect this analyst input. These are all issues that need to be considered when reviewing your PR and AR messaging. This includes any and all presentations made to the analysts and the press.

When it comes to the PR messaging review, don't let the fox guard the henhouse in selecting a reviewer. Select an objective messaging reviewer who has no ties with the group or groups they are reviewing. An outside consultant might be your best bet, particularly on the initial marketing alignment and messaging review. Whether you utilize an internal or external reviewer, the primary consideration is objectivity. This should not be a problem for anyone concerned, assuming they understand the importance of marketing alignment and how PR messaging relates to the overall alignment scheme.

## Sales and Partner Messaging

The sales group is probably the most likely offender when it comes to creating inconsistent messaging. The messaging alignment review process will have to include a thorough examination of all messaging that originates from the sales group. Being closer to the customers, it is conceivable that the messaging they are broadcasting is more in line with customer requirements than the messages coming from the marketing group. If a healthy dialogue existed between marketing and sales, this type of problem would and could be minimized. There are so many opportunities for the sales group to miscommunicate company or product messages. The odds of this happening are great. Depending on the type of products or services the company offers, the sales group may very well generate its own sales brochures, data sheets, competitive comparisons, case studies, success stories, proposals, etc. These are essential documents and should be available to the sales group, but that does not mean that they have to originate from within the sales group. And even if the sales group is given the responsibility of creating these documents, there should at least be a review process in place that requires approvals from the marketing group or the messaging coordinator during each stage of the creative process. Marketing has to be the clearinghouse and overseer of all company messaging, period. If consistency is to be maintained, then a centralized approval mechanism for content must be established and utilized. And as mentioned previously, marketing is the most appropriate group to have this responsibility.

There are instances when a member of the sales team has to create a document quickly and might not have time to take it through the approval cycle. It could mean a lost sale from a large customer. In such cases, if there is a tight relationship between all of the members of the marketing group and the sales group, this should not be a problem. If the communication and dialogue only occurs between the managers of these groups, then there is a potential for miscommunication. Even if the managers of both groups frequently exchange information, it might not be communicated clearly or effectively to their staff and the potential for inconsistency exists. So it is essential that all staff members have an opportunity to kibbutz with staff members from other departments and gain first-hand knowledge about company positioning and market requirements. It will also encourage "esprit de corps" and team building, which are very important to the success of the organization.

There are numerous opportunities for members of the sales group to send inconsistent messages or wrongly position products. During the review, any remotely located employees that have contact with customers or influencers should be examined as part of the messaging review. Outside salespersons are often located in areas far removed from corporate headquarters. In situations where they do not have the latest data sheets or brochures, they will improvise and create their own. In some cases, they call on customers directly; in other cases, they call on their sales channel partners, such as wholesalers, distributors, resellers, dealers, etc. If the sales collateral literature they create is only given to a small group of customers, then the messaging problem is minimized. However, if they distribute this literature to distributors or resellers who duplicate it and distribute it to their resellers or customers, then the problem is compounded. Sometimes, the outside sales reps place numerous requests for product data sheets, brochures, and other literature from the corporate marketing group, and the fulfillment just does not happen. In such cases, the salespersons have no alternative but to create their own sales materials and distribute it to their customers. Due to the isolation of these sales reps, there is also a good possibility that they are left out of the loop on new company and product developments, or initiatives pertaining to the company or products. This leads to additional inaccuracies and inconsistencies in the materials they create. With the advent of the Internet and inexpensive color printers, this problem should not exist at all. All company and product literature should be available online, and easily duplicated by remote sales reps.

If there is any animosity between marketing department management and sales department management, the odds of the sales group taking its own direction in messaging are increased. It is not only conceivable, but is more common in the corporate world than most CEOs would like to admit. Two big egos are at play here, and even with the intervention of the most senior management, they will still develop their own strategies concerning product positioning and messaging. If the heads of marketing and sales are at odds with each other, it is a foregone conclusion that the messaging emanating from each group will be different. Each person will believe that they have a better handle on what is going on in their market space and how best to articulate the product positioning and differentiation. It is not to say that each of these individuals might have a legitimate argument with regards to the direction that product positioning should take, but when a company sends messaging that is inconsistent, the market will not respond in the most positive manner. It is up to the CEO to nip this problem in the bud, and to make sure that every member of the management team is reading from the same page. The CEO is also responsible for ensuring that there is complete and total consensus among every member of the management team about the company's positioning and the product's positioning. Remember, mixed messages or inconsistent messages cause confusion in the market. Market confusion results in delayed sales, and in some cases, eliminates sales opportunities altogether.

The consultative selling approach is yet another area that can spawn inconsistent messaging. In using this approach, the salesperson listens carefully to the potential customer's objections and the customer's most salient requirements. Listening is certainly the key to successful communications, and this approach has proven to be successful for hundreds of companies. Just be sure to keep in mind that one customer's hot buttons do not necessarily represent the hot buttons of every customer. Do not develop sales collateral materials based on the input of one customer, even if they make a good case. Make sure that the features or benefits articulated as most important by your latest batch of customers match those that the marketing group believes to be important. If they do not, then it is time to get the marketing and sales group together for the purpose of bringing each other up to speed on changes in the market place. Once that is accomplished, then the determination can be made as to whether or not marketing should do additional market research to determine if the typical customer's current needs have changed. If, in fact, these needs have changed, make sure that this new information is

## Chapter Four: The Marketing Alignment Review Process

included and reflected in all of your company's marketing literature and sales collateral materials. Repeat after me...messaging consistency, messaging consistency, messaging consistency.

There are additional reasons for inconsistent messaging emanating from the sales group. This is most common in companies with direct sales forces. You know, where company salespersons deal directly with the customers. Because of their familiarity with the customers, the sales reps feel they are better equipped to articulate the customer's desires and requirements than their marketing counterparts. For example, if a sales rep for project management software hears numerous customers tell him or her that the product's biggest advantage is price, then that sales rep might use that knowledge to revise his pitch and emphasize price over all other product features. But what if the project management software is not the lowest-priced offering on the market—not even close? In this hypothetical example, the company's marketing group has positioned and promoted the product as "the best mid-range project management software value" on the market because the product offers more features than the majority of its competitors, yet is priced at the lower end of the price spectrum for mid-range project management software. So, in effect, product price is certainly an important component of the product's overall differentiation, but if the product were to be promoted only on its price alone, it would devalue the product and de-emphasize the breadth and depth of its features. A result of such messaging inconsistency would be reduced sales, revenue, and market share. And it is really the result of poor intra-departmental communications and interaction. This example illustrates just how vital it is for the sales and marketing teams to have alignment in their messaging. It could be difficult to recognize because the sales team could be achieving acceptable revenue from this product line without realizing that they could be producing more revenue with the proper messaging and positioning.

Your company's channel and other strategic partners represent another potential source for messaging inconsistency. This is just one more area for your messaging alignment review. They are also well positioned to broadcast inconsistent messaging. In fact, they are in a much better position than the company's employees to broadcast misinformation about a company and its products. Since the partner is not an integral division or department of the company, they are not privy to the latest market intelligence and competitive intelligence. In some cases, their partner company might only communicate with them via emails, training sessions, annual conferences, or other infrequently held events. Limited communications can easily result in messaging inconsistency. Certainly, the Internet can have a substantial impact on the improvement of these communications. And there are a number of software applications that have been made available in the last couple of years to improve partner relations and communications. Whatever methodology a company uses to reinforce, strengthen, and improve partner relations and communications will provide a significant return on the investment if: 1) the partner is truly strategic to the success of the product company; 2) the company takes full advantage of the methodology; 3) the company maintains solid bi-directional communications with the partner; and 4) the company monitors the activity and progress of the partner in reaching the mutually agreed upon objectives.

The two most important factors that will help the partner maintain consistent messaging regarding the company and its products are the Internet and face-to-face interaction with the partner. If the company develops and maintains its Web site properly, the partner should be able to access all of the information and tools required to accurately represent the company and its products. The very best way to build a relationship with an individual or an entity is through face-to-face contact. Personal relationships are key to business alliances. The most effective method of building such relationships is through personal contact. Channel partners need to feel comfortable selling someone else's products. In fact, if they do not feel comfortable selling a product, they will not do a good job at it. That means expectations and revenue goals are not met. The only way one can determine why a channel partner is not performing up to expectation is to visit that partner and find out what problems are contributing to the lackluster sales. And do not expect a channel partner to communicate on message, or achieve sales expectations, if their staff has not been adequately trained.

A personal example involves one of my previous employers, Artisoft, Inc. and one of their reseller channel partners, CompUSA. When I first went to work for Artisoft, I was the Major Accounts Manager. One of my clients was CompUSA. Their sales record with respect to Artisoft products was poor. My first step was to visit the corporate headquarters and meet with the product manager for network products. In reality, this person was responsible for several hundred additional products beside the

## Chapter Four: The Marketing Alignment Review Process 101

ones I represented. She really did not have a clue as to why Artisoft's products were doing so poorly. It should be mentioned that Artisoft at that time was growing very rapidly during this period. The sales revenue was almost doubling every year. Unfortunately, that was not the case at CompUSA. Artisoft's network products were coming in second to the products of a little-known company from England whose market share was less than fifty percent of Artisoft's nationally. My next step was to call on several CompUSA stores and meet with both the store managers and their sales people. Sometimes, it's best to go directly to the front line people, because they can tell you exactly why products are selling or not selling.

What I discovered was that the competitor's account manager was visiting each store every quarter, training their sales people on the advantages of her products, and providing CompUSA sales persons with a spiff, or cash incentive, for each unit they sold. She was also spreading misinformation about the functionality of the Artisoft products. In other words, the primary knowledge those sales people had received about the Artisoft product line was incorrect and damaging to its salability. My response was: 1) to initiate a national sales training program that articulated Artisoft product positioning, differentiation, and product advantages, while at the same time dispelling all of the misinformation about the Artisoft products; 2) to provide the CompUSA staff and sales people with abundant literature and competitive information; and 3) to implement a national spiff program to reward the salespeople for selling Artisoft products. Within six months, CompUSA had doubled its sales of Artisoft products and those products had displaced the competitor's products as the best-selling network products in all of the CompUSA stores nationwide.

There are three lessons to be learned from this experience. First, if your channel partner is not performing up to snuff, you are not necessarily going to learn why by making a phone call to their management or product marketing group. Go to the front lines and talk with the people that actually have to sell the products. I am not saying disrespect their management. How do you think I got approval to train all of those sales people and set up an incentive program? Establishing a good relationship with management is also very important.

Second, your competitors can be instrumental in assisting your channel partners in communicating misinformation about your company and its products. Most manufacturing companies would never think that their own distribution partners were sending out inconsistent or damaging messages about their company or products.

Third, do not be afraid to copy another vendor's methods for boosting sales, particularly if they have been effective in damaging the sales of your products. Turn the tables. If you have a superior product that is properly positioned and offers more advantages than your competitors, go for it! Do not underestimate the potential for inconsistent messaging by your channel partners when performing your messaging review.

## Training Group Messaging

The training group in your company is usually involved in training both new and seasoned employees on company direction, vision, initiatives, and policies, as well as providing product training to both employees and partners. In some instances, the training is informal. In other instances, the training is formal and structured. Your company's training programs provide numerous opportunities for misaligned messaging if the training courses are not designed with alignment in mind. This can be particularly troublesome when the training courses provided target external sales channel partners or total product solution partners. The last thing you want is training content that doesn't reflect your company and product positioning and value propositions. Make sure they are current and up to date. You cannot afford to send the wrong message to and through your partners. This is especially true if your partners are the primary conduits for the flow of company and product information to your target customers. It is hard enough to ensure that they're communicating the correct message when they interact with your customers. If your training doesn't equip them with the right message on the front end, there's no possibility that they will be able to communicate the real message when dealing with your targeted customers.

Depending on your organizational structure, training could be a separate department or departments. A company's training structure is typically based on the size of the company or the number of product divisions within the company. Training is normally associated with product lines. The more complicated or technical the product lines are, the more comprehensive the training programs will be. The targeted audiences for training generally include internal employees and external partners, including distribution and channel partners as well as total solution partners. If a training department exists, then monitoring and reviewing the training materials will be more straightforward and easier to manage. If, on the other hand, your training curriculum and materials are developed by employees in multiple departments, the job will be tougher. In some companies, the product management teams create the training curriculum and materials for their respective products or product lines. The sales group might create all of the training for the company's sales channel partners or outside reps. There could also be a training team in your human resources department responsible for training new employees on corporate policies and procedures. As you can see, coordinating the review of all training messaging could be quite a challenge based on how things are organized in your company.

Begin the process by reviewing all of your current training materials and curriculum and check for any possible alignment inconsistencies. If your company has several product lines or markets highly technical products, this process will be a big job. It has to be done. Apply as many resources to this job as you can afford. Once the initial review is completed, then you can incorporate the training messaging review into your overall marketing alignment process. Identifying alignment issues is job one during the initial review and ongoing monitoring activities. Review, analyze, and compare. Before any remediation can take place, you will have to prioritize the issues to be addressed and assign the most appropriate members of your team to repair these inconsistencies based on those priorities.

## Web site Messaging

Web site organization and content is a major contributor to corporate miscommunication and message inconsistency. During your messaging review, dedicate adequate resources for this part of the analysis. According to a recent survey of *CIO* and *Darwin* readers reported in the April 1, 2002 issue of *Darwin Online*, 37% of the readers believed their Web site's primary function was to provide specific product or account information. 34% believed the primary function of their Web site was to provide information about their company. Only 15% of those polled believed the purpose of their Web site was to buy, sell, or otherwise transact business. Approximately two-thirds of those surveyed believed their Internet sites were important or critical to their company's overall business strategy. What is probably most amazing is the fact that 32% of the respondents believed the Internet was of little or no importance. Moose hockey! Believe me now, and I will tell you later, the Internet is critical to the success of your business! Whether you use your Web site as a primary or secondary sales channel is dependent on your overall business strategy and the markets your company targets. Regardless, chances are very good that your customers will use your Web site to learn more about your company and the products it offers. In fact, there is a good chance that the first or initial contact a potential customer will have with your company will be through a visit to your Web site.

The first area to be concerned with is the navigational ease of your Web site. If potential customers, influencers, or partners cannot navigate the site easily and find what they are looking for in short order, game over. Your messaging is not terribly important if your audience never has the opportunity to see it. A word to the wise—make access as simple as possible. Remember that the more multimedia elements that are used in your Web site, the slower the site will take to load on a PC. Having a cutting-edge multimedia Internet site is not nearly as important as a high hit rate and minute drop-off wait. There are still a lot of folks out there with old PCs, dial-up connections, or slow modems. The faster your visitors can access your site, the less chance there will be of them dropping off. After all, if they do not see your messages, the messaging content is of no value. Just make sure that your Web site is easy to access, easy to navigate, has all of the right components, and reflects an accurate view of your company, its positioning, your product positioning, product differentiation, sales and distribution information, and all relevant information about your partners. And by all means, keep your Web site up to date. Every message on your Web site should mirror the content contained in your most current advertising, sales and marketing materials, customer success stories, case studies, white papers, current press releases, company announcements and events, channel partner and other partner initiatives, new customer or partner programs, etc. Your Web site is your window to the world.

Most customers and potential partners do all of their research on the Internet. It is imperative that your company has a Web site that reflects the size and importance of your company. In fact, a good Web site can do more to enhance the image and reputation of your company than virtually any other medium. At this point in time, you had better have a killer Web

## Chapter Four: The Marketing Alignment Review Process 105

site or your company's reputation and image will be diminished by a factor far exceeding the cost of developing and building that Web site. Not only will your Web site be a great source of information on your company, it can provide your company with a very significant sales channel. If you use the Web for your intranet, you can bring your remote employees, departments, divisions, channel partners, strategic suppliers, partners, and large customers much closer to all of the latest information and events pertaining to your company. With a great Web site, you can tell the world everything it needs to know about what's going on inside and outside your organization—instantaneously. You can keep in closer touch with your customers, the influencers, and your strategic partners. You can maintain control over all of your company and product messaging. This is why it will be an integral part of your messaging review. As validated in the April 2002 *Darwin* and *CIO* survey, your Web site is critical to the success of your business. Do not, I repeat, do not short-change your company's future by cutting corners in developing, building, and maintaining it.

Messaging is critical to establishing and maintaining the reputation and image of both your company and its products. Regardless of how your company is organized or structured, it is essential that you set up a message content monitoring system. Whether it is one person or a team, the function has to exist if you expect to achieve marketing alignment. This is not a "big brother" scenario. This person's job is not to judge or criticize the quality of the content, but only to ensure that the content is in alignment with corporate and product positioning and that it matches market expectations and requirements. With regard to the content of your channel partners and other strategic partners, the messaging content coordinator should only make suggestions. You cannot dictate content to third party partners. You can set up guidelines and you can make recommendations. It is important that each partner be brought up to speed on the role of marketing alignment and its positive impact on revenue and market share.

Initiate the alignment review analysis for messaging by answering the following questions:

1. Does your organization currently have a mechanism in place to review all corporate content, from executive presentations to advertising, sales and marketing collateral, press releases, training

materials, partner messaging and collateral materials, investor relations communications, Web site content, influencer presentations, etc.?

2. Has your CEO, VP of Marketing, or corporate communications manager communicated to all corporate divisions, departments, and employees the value of messaging alignment?

3. Are all facets of your current messaging in true alignment with corporate and product positioning?

4. Are all facets of your current messaging in true alignment with customer, influencer, and market requirements and expectations?

5. Do your press relations and analyst relations groups work closely with your marketing group when creating presentations or press releases?

6. Do your marketing group and sales group meet frequently to update each other on current customer and market trends?

7. If your sales group creates its own sales collateral materials, does marketing review it prior to release and distribution?

8. Are all of the sales group-created materials in true alignment with customer, influencer, and market requirements and expectations?

9. Does your marketing group meet with your channel and other strategic partners to discuss current customer and market trends?

10. Do your channel partners and other partners provide your marketing group with samples of the promotional and product collateral materials they create for the purpose of marketing and selling your products?

11. Are all of the sales, promotion, and product collateral materials used by your channel partners and other partners in true alignment with your product positioning and value proposition?

12. Are the curricula and materials used in product and corporate training classes reviewed by the marketing group or anyone else for proper alignment?

13. Are all of your company's training materials reviewed and updated regularly to incorporate any changes recently made to your company and product positioning and value propositions?

## Chapter Four: The Marketing Alignment Review Process         107

14. Does a group other than the marketing group administer your Web site? If so, who reviews and approves Web site content?

15. Is the Web site frequently updated to coincide with updates of company and product advertising and literature?

16. Is all of the Web site content in true alignment with company and product positioning? Does the Web site reflect current customer, influencer, and market requirements and expectations?

17. Does your company have a plan in place to coordinate the review of all messaging content for proper marketing alignment?

Once you have answered each question, you will understand exactly which areas need attention. List the areas requiring attention under the Messaging Section, rank order the issues, and then move on to the next section. After you complete all of the sections, you can go back and prioritize by section and the section's associated tasks, and the review process will be done.

### *Targeting*

Targeting is the last major element of your marketing alignment review process. Regardless of how successful your company is in developing its corporate and product positioning, sales strategies, or messaging, if your company misses its targets, even slightly, the rest is all for naught. You might believe that targeting is simply the result of your company and product positioning. In reality that is true, but your company can reach its targeted customer segment or segments without realizing the full potential of that segment or segments. Remember, targeting involves the selection of your partners, market influencers, as well. In reality, the customer segment or segments your company targets are directly related to the partners and market influencers you choose. The partners you select will determine if, indeed, you really reach your target market. The influencers you select will significantly impact your targeted customers' buying decisions. Choose the wrong influencers and the impact will be less than significant or, at worst, inconsequential. So even if you've done a terrific job in targeting the right market segment, you still have a lot of work to do in order to be successful and move towards market leadership.

During the product value proposition and positioning exercise, the customer segments most appropriate for your product or service offerings were established. Determining who is the right customer and reaching that specific customer segment is not always as easy as one might expect. Selecting the right partners and the right influencers is not always a slam-dunk, either. We will examine ways to ensure that there is alignment between the targeted customer segment(s) and your value proposition. Then the discussion will turn to how your organization can ensure that the partners you select match the customer segments you are targeting. And last, but not least, you will learn how to judge the appropriateness of the influencers you are targeting. Even though the targeted customer segment or segments are the last element of the marketing alignment diagram, we will begin with them first. In reality, these segments were determined on the front-end during the development of the product value proposition. Targeting is more about ensuring that your sales and marketing elements reach these segments. By the way, throughout this text, the terms customer segment and market segment will be interchangeable. So do not be confused when market segment is used in place of customer segment or vice versa. This portion of the alignment review process is all about validating your positioning and sales strategies with your targeted customer segments, influencers, and partners.

## Targeting Customer Segments

Let's review the process your company should have used in targeting the most appropriate customer segment. During the development of your product's value proposition, you identified the customers that would be most receptive to your product's application or solution, as well as the distinct advantages your product has over its competitors. As you remember, I pointed out that there would be another decision to make at this juncture. That decision involved whether or not you believed it would be more prudent to target a narrower customer segment instead of targeting the larger overall market. The criteria upon which you base this decision will involve a couple of very important factors.

First, you should have ascertained if your product has major advantages over the competition that could be easily articulated and that would create a must-buy attitude in the mind of the potential customers. If the answer to that question was yes, your next step should have been to deter-

## Chapter Four: The Marketing Alignment Review Process

mine if this applied to the total population of that market segment. In other words, would your product appeal to the whole market? Maybe you determined that there was a narrower market segment for which your product would have greater appeal. If you determined that your product would appeal to the larger overall market, there was another factor to consider prior to finalizing your target market. That factor had to do with whether or not your organization had the resources to compete successfully against the market leaders of the target market. If you determined that your product would appeal to the overall market and your company had adequate resources to compete against the market leaders, then that approach should have been taken. All of this was validated and reinforced by your extensive market research.

If, on the other hand, you determined that your value proposition would be more compelling to a narrower market segment, then you should have targeted that customer segment. If you believed that the market leaders were so powerful that they could dispel your advantage by virtue of their market domination and stature, then you should have chosen the niche or narrower segment of the market. If you chose a narrower segment or sub-segment of the market, did you determine the specialized product requirements necessary to be competitive in that market and revise your product accordingly? Such modifications should have made your product so compelling that it is a must-have item in your targeted market space. Review your product and targeting strategy to ensure that you have taken the correct approach in customer targeting. Be sure that you have enough market research and customer data to back up the market requirements and validate your go-to-market strategy.

Targeting a sub-segment or niche of an overall market prior to expansion into the larger overall market has been successfully accomplished by hundreds of companies. Ping, Inc. founder, Karsten Solheim, began his golf club company by targeting a sub-segment of the golf market, the putter market segment, in 1959. In fact, like Mr. Hewlett and Mr. Packard, Solheim began his company in his garage. In 1969, Mr. Solheim added irons to his Ping product line and expanded his target market. Now the company produces a full line of golf clubs and golf products, and is one of the most successful golf club manufacturers in the world. New Balance Athletic Shoe, Inc. began life in 1900s by offering custom-made arch supports. In 1930, New Balance offered its first running shoe. Today, New Balance offers athletic shoes for running, cross training, basketball, soccer, tennis, and numerous other applications. New Balance not only markets all types of athletic and hiking shoes, they also offer fitness and athletic apparel. Another example of starting a business by targeting a niche segment of the market is Cannondale, the American bicycle manufacturer. Cannondale began its business in 1971 by introducing the bicycle industry's first bicycle trailers. The company grew from there by adding cycling apparel and accessory lines. In 1983, Cannondale introduced its first bicycle. The company's first bicycle model was highly differentiated from the steel models that dominated the industry in that it was an all-aluminum model that was lighter and more flexible than its competitors. Today, Cannondale offers over 80 models of bicycles in more than 60 countries.

There have also been instances where mainstream market competitors have taken products with mass-market appeal, and customized those products to have greater appeal to a sub-segment of the market. These companies have done this for the purpose of expanding their market reach. This is defined as market segmentation. A recent example of this comes from the company that produces Bayer Aspirin, Bayer AG. They are now offering a version of Bayer Aspirin with an additional ingredient—calcium. This product targets women over the age of forty. Aspirin is known to help reduce heart disease when taken daily. Calcium is known to help combat osteoporosis in women over forty. By combining aspirin and calcium, Bayer determined this combination would appeal to this specific market segment.

Market segmentation is a smart way to offer differentiation whether your company is a start-up or a market leader. Another example would be Teddy Grahams from RJR Nabisco. We all grew up with the familiar Graham crackers from Nabisco. Nabisco knew that parents had been buying these crackers for their children for many years. They wanted to establish brand identification and demand with the kids themselves. They also wanted to further differentiate themselves from all of the other companies that sold Graham crackers. So they introduced a new line of graham crackers shaped like teddy bears. Teddy Grahams has been a smashing success and has expanded Nabisco's popularity in the children's market segment.

It is not necessary to remain in the original market segment that was targeted when a product or brand begins life. Products can evolve and target customer segments altogether different from the original markets that

## Chapter Four: The Marketing Alignment Review Process

they targeted. Consider Subaru, the Japanese automaker. When Subaru first began importing cars to the United States in late 1960s, its primary market target was sub-compact economy market segment. This segment's primary requirements were a cheap purchase price and great gas mileage. These cars were really small compared to present day models. They were smaller than the original VW Beetles. The VW Beetles were their competition, along with the other newly arrived Japanese imports. In most cases, Subaru buyers could barely afford these inexpensive mini-cars. Typical buyers were young first-time car buyers who wanted to buck the prevailing trends. Today, Subaru targets older, more affluent buyers. The target market includes young to middle-aged upwardly mobile professionals that are more interested in superbly engineered vehicles that offer all-wheel drive. Economy is secondary to these individuals. As Subaru's product line has evolved and grown up, so has their target market. Subaru's primary competition, VW, Toyota, Honda, Mazda, and Nissan have matured in a similar fashion. Part of this evolution has to do with Japan's emphasis on engineering and quality, and part of it has to do with the changing requirements of the market. The market has evolved and grown up, and so have the Japanese automakers.

Hopefully, when you identified the most appropriate customer segments to target, you chose those that matched your value proposition and the go-to-market resources you had available at that time. Market segmentation is a good, viable strategy for entering a new market or for expanding your market reach in your existing market. Customers in market segments have different requirements that are more specialized than those in the mass market. Make the appropriate modifications to your product so that it is better equipped than your competitors to meet those specialized requirements of the market niche. Not just a little better, but a lot better than the competition. Regardless of which path you take, it is essential that your product's value proposition create a powerful must-have or must-buy attitude in the minds of the customers you are targeting. Me-too products do not have a chance in any market unless that market is reaching the end of its life cycle, and you can offer those products at a price that is 30-40% lower than that of the market leader. At that point in time, the market has become commoditized, and price will be a differentiating factor worth pursuing. Of course, you'd better act quickly, because the market will not be viable for very long.

Assuming you identified and targeted the most appropriate customer segments for your product or products, the next step would have been to develop your go-to-market and launch strategies and tactics. To do this, your product or marketing teams should have properly identified the exact demographic profile of your targeted customer. Hopefully, your team learned everything possible about your targeted customers. The critical requirement in such a profile includes information concerning age, gender, median income, job or profession types, shopping preferences, media preferences, sales channel preferences, geographic dispersion and concentrations, and any other factors that impact the buying decision process. This information should have been gathered when you were validating your product's value proposition. Surveying potential customers, as mentioned earlier in this book, should give you all of the information you need to build the profile. If you required more, then you should have done a second survey and any additional market research necessary to pull the requisite information together. Your go-to-market strategy and tactics should have been based on this information. The accuracy and completeness of this research would have given you the exact information needed reach the exact customers you were targeting. In most cases, you only have one opportunity to get this right, and hopefully, you did. Actually, if you did not do it right the first time, sometimes you have additional opportunities to perform this exercise again as your product and your market evolve and change. We will make the assumption that you did a reasonable job in targeting and profiling, given the fact that you probably would not be reading this book if your company was not still in business.

## Targeting Channel Partners

Targeting partners primarily involves selecting your channel partners and/or whole product model partners. First of all, selecting business partners is kind of like selecting your employees. Your partners had better be strategic to your success and in alignment with your goals, values, and direction, or you've been wasting precious resources that can't be recovered. Unless your company has unlimited resources, mistakes are not a viable option in this exercise. Also keep in mind that 'unlimited resources' is not a term that is part of the vocabulary of your venture capitalists, investors, or shareholders. So you had better be very selective and discriminating in choosing your partners. The employee analogy is closer

## Chapter Four: The Marketing Alignment Review Process

to the truth than you might think. Your partners are an extension of your organization. They play an integral part in your success or failure. They are also in a perfect position to destroy your image or reputation. Conversely, they can enhance your image and reputation if you choose them wisely.

Sales channel partners are necessary for any company that does not intend to sell its own products. Most product companies use some type of distribution structure to sell their products. It could be through wholesalers, distributors, and/or targeted resellers. When you developed your value proposition, you validated this proposition by surveying customers you believed would be your target market, so you already know a great deal about your targeted customers. Achieving alignment with your channel partners meant locating and partnering with those resellers that target the same customer segments. It would be less than prudent to consider any resellers that are not targeting the customer segments you have identified for your products. In fact, when you set your sales strategies, you profiled the exact types of channel partners that you would be targeting. In some cases, your channel partners will be wholesalers or distributors, who sell to the resellers you believe are most appropriate in reaching your targeted customer segments. Depending on the current market trends, you might be selling directly to the resellers.

Regardless of whether you are selecting distributors or resellers, the process will be the same. You should have profiled the structure you believe to be the most appropriate distribution mechanism for your products. With this profile in mind, you should have conducted phone conversations or face-to-face meetings with the prospective channel partners that met your requirements. During this process, you should have been able to quickly determine if they met your requirements and if you met theirs. Important considerations would have included their enthusiasm and motivation with regard to your product's value proposition. If they do not buy into your vision and your product's promise, how can they possibly sell your products? Assuming that they did share your enthusiasm about your product's potential, then you should have discussed their selling approach and mutual revenue goals. If there was agreement on this front, then you were almost home free. Of course, there are other important points of negotiation such as terms, stocking levels, promotional policies, training policies, co-op advertising terms, return policies, support policies, and so forth. If the prospective channel partner met your initial requirements, then you should have been able to resolve these other issues without any major problems. Review your approach in channel partner selection and determine if all the specified steps were taken.

When assembling the sales channel partner group, it is essential to make sure you have done your homework and have an accurate appraisal of the revenue-generating potential of your sales channel partners. You have to ensure that your channel partners can provide your company with the geographic coverage you believe necessary to adequately reach your targeted customer segments. You have to develop a comprehensive training program for your channel partner's sales team. And you will need to establish a system for the timely distribution of the sales collateral materials that your partners require to be informed and up-to-date. If your products require any technical knowledge or expertise to sell, you will not be successful unless you have effectively trained your sales partners' salespeople and continually keep them up to date on the latest product information.

Salespeople sell products they feel comfortable selling, period. If they do not feel competent to sell your products, they will not consider selling them. If they are selling hammers or lipstick, a comprehensive training program will not be necessary. There are situations where you are using mass merchants to sell somewhat technical or complex products. In these instances, it is critical to your success that the salespersons selling your products have the basic information and resources required to sell these types of products. If you remember the CompUSA example I mentioned earlier in this chapter, then it should be apparent that I learned this lesson first hand. In addition to CompUSA, several other mass merchants were selling the product line that I was responsible for at that time. Their sales people did not know squat about networking products either. I had no choice but to develop training materials that simplified the task of selling complex, technical products without having any real expertise or knowledge about these products. Quick reference charts and informative packaging were part of the solution—training that offered just enough information on features, benefits, competitive advantages, and other very basic information. Too much information will scare your potential sales champions away from your offerings. And it worked. Don't wait for their eyes to glaze over during your training session. Less is more. Information overload is a very real possibility in such a scenario.

## Chapter Four: The Marketing Alignment Review Process

In the late 1980s, I was a product manager at Computer Associates for a line of microcomputer accounting software products. At that time, Egghead Software was a thriving software retail chain with a couple of hundred stores spread out across the country. We had just signed a very large distribution agreement with Egghead to carry the accounting product line that I managed. Their salespersons were typically fresh out of high school and certainly not well versed on accounting principals or bookkeeping. If you wanted to see them dive for cover, just walk into any of their stores and ask them to explain the differences between the accounting software products they had for sale. Remember what I have said about salespeople selling only those products they are comfortable with? What's a mother to do?

Well, Virginia, you give them a cheat sheet that they can keep with them while they're at the store. I created a tri-fold quick reference chart that would fit easily in a shirt pocket. This quick reference chart contained all the basic information the salesperson would need to field questions about the various accounting modules. Next, I arranged a number of training sessions at their larger outlets. The training only included the most basic accounting information and was more about features, benefits, and competitive advantages. I then established a Mystery Shopper Program. The premise of this program was to send an unidentified Mystery Shopper into randomly selected stores located in different regions of the country. The shopper would ask a few questions that identified themselves as a potential customer for our product—the CA accounting software product. If the store sales rep recommended an accounting module from my product line, the Mystery Shopper would hand that sales rep two crisp one hundred dollar bills on the spot. Then we would photograph that person and put his or her picture in the Egghead Store Internal Newspaper. Guess what? My product line outsold all of the other accounting software products at Egghead Stores nationwide. Help the sales people feel comfortable about selling your products and then give them incentives sell more. It worked.

Targeting the best possible channel partners is all about fit. Your partners will have to target the most appropriate segments, and they will have to use a sales approach in keeping with your product offerings, and your company's values and vision. Your partners will have to clearly understand and buy into your product's positioning, differentiation, and value proposition. They will need to be receptive to your training. Your channel partners will have to be enthusiastic and on board with all of your channel and promotional marketing programs. And they will have to provide your company with the geographic coverage and revenue-generating potential necessary to achieve your revenue and market share goals. In reviewing your current channel partners, do they meet all of the criteria listed above?

## Targeting Total Product Solution Partners

Targeting total product solution partners is mandatory if your product is not a total solution by itself. First, you must create a whole or total product solution model. This model is basically a picture of the complete solution of which your product is a part. It will include every product and every service required for the total solution of which your product is an integral part. For example, if your company sells personal computer disk drives, your product is useless without a personal computer. This is not to say that you could not sell them separately through computer or electronic stores. You could. But there are issues of compatibility, installation, and software that have to be addressed. And you would be considerably more successful if your disk drives were endorsed, recommended, and/or bundled with branded personal computers. It is very important to your success to partner with personal computer manufacturers and software vendors. Maybe even cable vendors, if some or all of your disk drives are external and not internal devices. And there is a service component needed if you plan to offer onsite service nationwide. If your product were the total solution, then you would not need partners to help you complete the solution. Total solution partners are generally complementary product vendors, and in some cases, service or support organizations, depending on the complexity of the total solution.

An example of this type of partnering would be Nokia. Nokia is certainly a market leader. Nokia did not become the largest manufacturer of cell phones in the world without some help. Cell phones are useless without the cellular service provider such as AT&T, Sprint, Voicestream, Cingular, etc. Offering a multitude of models with features for virtually every application has made Nokia the cell phone of choice. Removable, designer faceplates added to their popularity. But the single most important factor in their success has been the partnering with a wide variety of geographically dispersed service providers. Bose car stereos represent

Chapter Four: The Marketing Alignment Review Process       117

another successful model for partnering. There are a gaggle of car stereo manufacturers in existence. But Bose is the most popular factory-installed stereo system used in upscale sports cars, sports coupes, sedans, and luxury cars. Not only does that partnering increase Bose car stereo sales, it also enhances the company's image very significantly. Such alliances are the essence of total product solution partnering.

Total product solution partnering, when done correctly, will increase your company's revenue, enhance your company's and product's image, and expose your brand to more potential customers than your company could expect without these partnerships. So what should you look for in a total product solution partner? The same qualities your company would look for in a channel partner and more. Prospective total solution partners should share your company's values, vision, and direction. Their sales approach should be in keeping with your own. They should be targeting the same customer segments. Potential partners should have equivalent or larger sales and marketing organizations. Their geographic reach should be equivalent or larger than your own. Their revenue-generating capabilities should be in keeping with your own. In fact, the most attractive partners would be companies with greater potential than your own. You could go too far in this regard. If your partner's volume potential is way beyond your manufacturing or distribution capabilities, your reputation could be damaged beyond repair if you fail to meet demand for any length of time. Or maybe your company would have to compromise its quality in order to keep up with the demand. It sounds like the best kind of problem to have, right? It is not. Your company's image and reputation would be seriously tainted in such a situation and your company will lose out in the end. Just think win/win when reviewing the total product solution partners that you have already chosen or that you are considering. They should be your peers, the fit should be right on the money, and both companies should share equally in the success.

## Targeting Influencers

Targeting influencers is a subject that most businesses do not give serious consideration to when developing their overall business and marketing plans. This is a curious phenomenon given the impact these individuals have on your company's success. Influencers include journalists, analysts, and thought leaders who cover a specific market space. The nature or type of products offered by a company is certainly a determining factor as to the relative importance of these influencers. Consumer products are not nearly as susceptible to the opinions of influencers as are business products. Expensive consumer products such as automobiles, appliances, electronics products, and computers are more susceptible to the opinions of the influencers. Business or industrial products and solutions that are sold to corporate America are very susceptible to influencer opinions. In fact, they can easily determine your survival in your respective markets. If you've been in your respective industry for any length of time, you know exactly how important the influencers are to the success of your company and its products. If the influencers have no impact on your company's success, you can skip this section. Otherwise, keep reading.

The best example of the power of the influencers probably relates to companies that sell into the Fortune 500 or Global 1000 corporations. In this arena, the most important influencers are typically the analyst firms. If a company sells enterprise software, hardware, or communications systems, there is an analyst firm that covers that product market. Your targeted customers subscribe to these analyst firms and rely on their input to determine exactly what technologies to implement, when to implement them, and what products should be used in that implementation. If the analysts who cover your market do not bless your products or solutions, your company and its products will not even make the short list of the corporate decision makers. That is why companies like IBM, Oracle, Compaq, Sun Microsystems, Microsoft, and others spend hundreds of thousands of dollars on their analyst relations programs. An analyst's recommendation can determine the success of a company in this type of market.

Journalists and editors for publications that cover mid-market products and solutions have similar power over business-to-business products and solutions. An Editor's Choice Award or Product of the Year Award by a trade publication usually equates to more revenue generated by the recipient. Think about the value of a *Motor Trend* magazine "Car of the Year Award" or a *Consumer Reports* "Highest Rated Product" award. Those types of reviews and awards are money in the bank. Journalist and editors can make or break companies in all types and sizes of markets just by their virtue of their product review or exclusion. Never underestimate the power of the press when it comes to making products successful. You

## Chapter Four: The Marketing Alignment Review Process 119

should have a clear understanding of the influencers in your market space. The real question here is what programs have been initiated by your organization to influence those who influence your markets and potential customers?

Targeting influencers is zero sum game. You only have a certain amount of resources to devote to them, so you had better make sure that you are targeting the most influential members of the press and analyst communities. Too many companies take the shotgun approach and target every journalist, analyst, and thought leader they can uncover. Not the best approach. Why would you devote resources to influencers who have little or no effect on your targeted customer segments? The most effective approach is to first identify the main influencers in your market space, and then rank order them according to some specific parameters. These parameters include overall market coverage, primary market focus, overall exposure, exposure to your customer segments, and influence with regard to both the overall market and your specific customer segments. Accessibility should be a consideration only if the analyst, journalist, or thought leader is inaccessible. Once you have rank ordered these influencers, then you should select the top five, ten, or fifteen. The number targeted will be based on the amount of resources you have available to devote to each one. Invest your money where you will get the best return.

In looking at those who influence your market space, there are some other influencers that will affect your image and reputation in the market place who do not fall into easily definable influencer categories. They are not journalists or analysts. They could be considered thought leaders. These influencers can be friendly or hostile. And there is nothing you can do to change their view of you if they are hostile. These influencers come from your competitors and your competitors' channel partners. Most dominant market leaders' management team members are considered experts in their respective markets or market segments. If they compete in your market, then they will be considered an expert and influencer in your market space. They are often asked for opinions or expert commentary on events that shape their markets. The channel partners of these market leaders are in similar positions of power. In most cases, there is not much you can do in terms of building relationships with these guys since they play for the opposing team. Of course if one of your channel partners is in such a position, then that's a different story. You very well might be able to get a favorable report or comment about your company from such a partner. That's about as far as it goes. Building relationships with your partners is an essential ingredient of the partnership, so the opportunity is there. Also, keep in mind that if you have total solution partners that are considered market leaders in their respective markets, you could possibly benefit from their influence as well.

Initiate the alignment review analysis for targeting by answering the following questions:

## *Questions on Customer Targeting*

1. Does the customer segment your product targets match your company and product positioning, as well as your product value proposition?
2. Could you segment your target market and achieve more share?
3. Do your product's differentiation and competitive advantages create a must-buy attitude in the minds of your targeted customer segments?
4. What are the market leaders doing in response to your strategy and tactics? Is it impacting your growth potential?
5. Will your company ever be a market leader in the market your company is targeting?
6. Does your company have the resources to effectively compete with the market leaders?
7. Is the customer segment you're currently targeting the most lucrative of the segments you could be targeting with regard to: a) revenue potential, b) growth potential, and c) cost of sales?
8. Have you updated the demographic profile of your targeted customer segments recently to ensure your marketing strategies and tactics are still appropriate? If so, have you made the appropriate changes to your products, as well as in your approach and tactics?

## *Questions on Channel Partner Targeting*

1. Does your channel structure reflect your channel strategy exactly?

# Chapter Four: The Marketing Alignment Review Process

2. Does your channel structure reflect your company and product positioning?
3. Do your channel partners target the same customer segments that your company targets?
4. Do your channel partners use the same sales and marketing approach that you advocate for your products?
5. Do your channel partners share your company's values, vision, and direction?
6. Are all of your channel partners together capable of achieving your revenue and market share objectives?
7. Do your channel partners provide the geographic reach required to capture all of the potential customers in all of the regions you have targeted?
8. Are your channel partners receptive to your training?
9. Do your channel partners take advantage of all of your sales and marketing collateral?
10. Do they buy into and broadcast your product's value proposition verbatim?
11. Is their messaging in true alignment with your own?
12. Do your channel partners have all of the tools necessary to do an effective job of marketing and selling your products?
13. Do you initiate frequent and ongoing dialogue with your channel partners to learn and understand what is going on out in the field?
14. Should you consider adding new channel partners or eliminating poor performing channel partners?
15. Are their new channels that you could add that would increase your exposure, sales, and market share?

## *Questions on Total Solution Partner Targeting*
1. Do you need total solution partners? If not, skip these questions.

2. Have you constructed a total product model that reflects every product and service required to make your offering a viable solution?
3. Have you recruited and secured all of the total solution partners required to provide the total solution of which your product is a part?
4. Do your total solution partners target the same customer segments?
5. Are your total solution partners' value propositions in alignment with your company's value propositions?
6. Are your total solution partners' messaging in alignment with your own?
7. Are they receptive to bundling, co-branding, or co-marketing?
8. Are your total solution partners market leaders? Are they similar in size and resources to your company?
9. Is your relationship with your total solution partners truly a partnership or do they dictate the terms and conditions of the relationship?
10. Do your total solution partners provide you with leverage in the market place? Do they enhance your image or detract from it?
11. Are there additional total solution partners in other product areas that you could add that would increase your exposure, your revenue, and your market share?

## *Questions on Influencer Targeting*
1. Do members of the press or analyst communities play a role in your customer's buying decisions?
2. Do you need to have an influencer relations program?
3. If so, do you currently have one in place?
4. Have you identified the influencers who have the most significant impact on your target markets?

## Chapter Four: The Marketing Alignment Review Process

5. Have you rank ordered all of the influencers that impact your market?
6. Have you initiated a plan to build relationships with only the top five, ten, or fifteen influencers based on the resources available? Have you implemented that plan?
7. Are your influencer communications and presentations in alignment with your company and product positioning, value propositions, and overall messaging?
8. Are you providing the influencers with just the information they need or are you trying to market to them?
9. Are you communicating frequently with the most influential journalists, analysts, and thought leaders in your market space?
10. Do you receive competitive intelligence from the influencers in your space?
11. Have you gotten quantifiable results from your influencer relations program up to this point?
12. Do you have any channel partners that are considered experts on your market space? If so, have you built a solid relationship with them?
13. Do you have any total solution partners that are considered experts in your chosen market segment? If so, have you built a solid relationship with them?

Once you have answered each question, you will understand exactly which areas need attention. List the areas requiring attention under the Targeting Section, rank order the primary issues, and move on to the final review process. After you complete all of the sections, you can go back and prioritize each section and its associated tasks, and the review process will be done.

### *The Overall Alignment Review Process*

Prior to beginning the marketing alignment review process, you have to determine who is going to carry out this review. Will it be you and your management team? Will it be a team assembled from your internal staff?

Or will the team be made up of staff members from a third party consulting firm? This decision is as critical as the review itself. It is critical because if you choose an outside organization to perform this review and they do not have the experience and background to do this type of analysis and/or perform the overall alignment, then you're wasting your time and money. Make sure that you do not approach this selection process lightly because your company's future may well depend on the outcome of this project. Get references, do the math, and calculate the ROI. It is important that you establish some type of metrics for measuring the success of this exercise and the return on your investment, whether it is internally or externally staffed. After all, your company's future is on the line!

Once you have assembled the marketing alignment review team, it's time to go to work. After you or your appointed alignment team members have gone through each section of the marketing alignment review and answered all of the questions pertaining to each section, it's time to evaluate the results of your findings and begin the final alignment review process. Because the first two sections, corporate positioning and product positioning, profoundly influence the other alignment components, it is not only advisable but it is imperative that you begin the alignment review process by examining your answers to the questions posed in those sections. Begin at the top and work your way down the list.

Prioritize the unsatisfactory answers in section one and then in section two. Unsatisfactory answers are those that will require strategy revisions. In most cases, the issues in section one should be addressed first. There could be instances where revisions affecting section two will require similar revisions in section one. Typically, your products are a reflection of your company's direction, values, and vision. However, if there are significant events or trends coming from your chosen market, you might have to revise your product set to accommodate those changes, and then make corresponding changes in your company's positioning. This is the exception to the rule, but it might be necessary for survival if you are competing in a highly dynamic market. Once you have identified the issues and challenges facing your company with regard its corporate and product strategies, you will know where the alignment process needs to begin. Addressing those issues will be your first step towards achieving true alignment.

Sales channel strategies, messaging, and targeting will be addressed once remediation is completed in the corporate and product strategy

## Chapter Four: The Marketing Alignment Review Process

areas. In fact, if there are significant changes to the your corporate and product strategies, it will most likely be necessary to revisit the questions relating to sales strategies, messaging, and targeting. The original answers were not based on the new strategies. Consequently, you will have to go back and recheck your answers to those questions and make sure they are still valid. Once that task is accomplished, you can begin prioritizing the issues in sections three, four, and five. The remediation process will be based on the amount of work involved in realigning the misaligned elements. If the majority of your alignment elements are in line, then the work will be minimal. On the other hand, if the elements are in total disarray, then you will have a great deal of work to do. We will get into the details of the remediation process in the next chapter.

# CHAPTER FIVE

# THE MARKETING ALIGNMENT REMEDIATION PROCESS

Remediation is the fix. If your sales and marketing elements are out of alignment, then you will have to fix these problems. This means that you will have to examine each alignment element, determine the changes required to bring that element back into alignment, and make those changes. This is not necessarily brain science or rocket surgery. Actually, it is rocket science if you don't understand the concepts of marketing alignment. If, in fact, you have reached this point in the book and you still do not understand the concepts of sales and marketing alignment, then go directly to the establishment where you purchased this book and demand a full refund. Do not pass go and do not try to collect your $200. Of course, you won't be getting a refund, but it might make you feel better. Then again, maybe you should go back and reread chapters one through four.

In performing the remediation, you will need to first assemble the remediation team. In selecting the remediation team members, remember that any remediation involving the first two components will require your management team. Key members of your executive team should undertake corporate and product positioning. No other staff members would be appropriate for this task. A high-level management team should also undertake sales channel strategies. Messaging alignment remediation will require members of your product management group and your marketing team. The staff members most closely tied to your channel partners, your total solution partners, and your market influencers should carry out targeting remediation. The remediation activities will in large part determine your company's success in its chosen markets. Do not take this exercise lightly. It will have a major impact on your company's success or failure. Do it right, and your chances of becoming a market leader will increase substantially.

Set up a meeting to discuss assignments and time lines. Print and hand out your findings from the marketing alignment review to every staff member involved prior to the meeting. Prioritize the required remediation tasks based on addressing the strategic elements first, and the tactical elements second. Prioritize the tasks within each of these categories. Assign responsibilities for the remediation tasks to the appropriate staff members. If your review revealed alignment issues relating to your corporate positioning and/or product positioning and value propositions, you will have to address those issues immediately. If you have to make any major changes in your corporate or product positioning, you will need to revisit and possibly restart the alignment review for the other elements. Sales channel strategies, messaging, and targeting will all be affected by any changes made to your corporate and/or product positioning.

Agree to meet once the remediation is complete to discuss the process, any unforeseen issues, and your team members' thoughts on the overall process. Then ask each member of the team about his or her perception of the marketing alignment and the success of the team's remediation efforts. You will want to devise a system of metrics for measuring the results. The metrics will be based on revenue growth and market share growth. You will also need to measure the associated reductions in marketing costs related to revenue gains. Measure the success of the alignment activities quarterly. You should expect to see measurable results within two quarters of the initial remediation.

This is a serious business process and will, to a large extent, determine your company's success in its chosen market. I am sure that you want to increase your revenue and market share. And you want to reduce your marketing expenses as a percentage of your revenue. So let's get this process started and get a head start on your competition. The first two elements of marketing alignment are strategic and the rest are tactical. Since your sales and marketing tactics are based on your overall strategy, the most sensible place to begin remediation will be your company's strategic elements. Let's begin, shall we?

## Start with the Strategic Elements

### The Corporate Positioning Statement

If your corporate positioning does not reflect the current values, vision, and direction of your company, this will be the starting point for the remediation process. You and your management team will have tackle this project first. That means that you and your team will have to go in and fix it so it does reflect those attributes of your organization. That will be the first step in the remediation process. Some of you might be thinking: "How can anyone start a business and not incorporate their company's values, direction, objectives, vision, and competitive advantage into their corporate positioning statement?" It is possible. It is more likely that over the years your direction or your vision could have changed course to reflect the changing dynamics of the markets within which you compete or new product directions that your company has taken. Generally, people's values do not change, so that is not an area we will examine in this process. And if your values have changed, let us hope those changes are positive in nature and will impact your company and its leadership in a very good way.

The first step in revising your corporate positioning is to take a look back. Determine exactly where you have come from and where it is you intend to go with your company. Take a minute and write down your company's strengths and weaknesses—at its inception and as of today. Compare the differences. Such a retrospective is important in understanding the changes that have taken place over the past few years and why your company responded to these changes as it did. This will help you understand your company's current position in the market and give you the insights needed to steer your company in a more defined direction in the future. Take a look at the events, trends, and forces that have and will be influencing the direction and nature of your markets over the next couple of years. In this day and time, long-term planning with regard to corporate strategy and positioning is not a viable alternative. Your corporate positioning will have to become more chameleon-like and change with the market. Your values and your vision for the company can be fixed, but your company's direction, strategy, and tactics will have to accommodate the dynamics of the market. Think about the Subaru example and that company's evolution. When reinventing your corporate positioning statement, keep that in mind.

Your corporate positioning has to clearly differentiate your company from your competitors. Like your company's market or markets, your competition is not static. So change is inevitable...for them, for you. If you can develop a corporate positioning statement that is somewhat malleable, then it will be more responsive to change. There should be some basic tenets in your corporate positioning that will remain unchanged even when the market and/or your competitors change. Things like customer service, quality, or value are areas with which your company can align itself as part of your corporate positioning. Dell Computer's corporate positioning has not changed dramatically over the years even though the PC market, traditional PC selling channels, and Dell's competitors have changed dramatically. Dell's model has always been to sell direct to its customers. Their selling channel has evolved from direct response magazine ads to mail order catalog sales and telemarketing, and today uses the Internet as their primary sales channel. Dell's computers are still built to the customer's specifications. Their promise of local service is still part of their customer promise, even if some of the service is provided via the Internet these days. So you do not necessarily change your business model, which is a reflection of your corporate positioning, but you will have to adapt that model to the changing requirements of your customers and the market.

Your corporate positioning statement will still have to clearly state what it is your company does, how it does this, how your company is different from the rest of your competitors, and why it is better—your competitive advantage, and your company's basic value proposition. If it does not reflect each and every one of these components, you will need to update it so that each item is clearly, succinctly, and accurately represented and articulated. Schedule a meeting to sit down with your executive team and redraft it. There are two additional, highly important requirements that will have to be met in recreating this document.

The first requirement in revising your corporate positioning statement is nailing down your company's value proposition and ensuring that it is still appropriate for the current market conditions. Just like the value proposition for each of your products, your corporate positioning has to clearly articulate that undisputable claim that differentiates your company from the other companies in your market space. This claim is your com-

## Chapter Five: The Marketing Alignment Remediation Process

pany's competitive advantage. It has to create a must-buy attitude in the mind of your prospective customers. And this competitive advantage has to be intuitively obvious to the most casual observer.

David Olgivy, the father of American advertising, states in his book *Olgivy on Advertising* that if a farmer in Iowa can't understand the message you're trying to convey, then rewrite it until he can. This has to be a claim that cannot be attributable to your competitors. If any one of your competitors can even falsely claim a similar advantage with any credibility at all, then your claim will be lost in the confusion. You will have to rethink and redraft your value proposition. Admittedly, that does not necessarily make sense, but look at it this way. Unless you're already the market leader, you're the new guy on the block. Let's say you make claim A. The dominant market leader in your space has immediate credibility because of its stature, brand equity, and track record in the market. That simply means they can make a similar claim and the majority of potential customers in your market space will believe it. Consequently, your claim will have to be clearly different and undisputable.

The second requirement for your corporate positioning statement has to do with brevity. You have to be able to relate it to a total stranger in the time it takes to ride an elevator up a few floors. If you cannot do this, then you should get your executive staff together and redraft this document. Bring in a wordsmith if necessary. If explaining the basic premise of your business strategy requires a long-winded oratory, then you do not have a good understanding of your company's value proposition or strategic position in the market. Most venture capitalists will tell you that if you cannot accurately and concisely describe what your company does and its competitive advantage in that amount of time, then you really do not have a clue about your company's true positioning in the market place. That also means that they would not consider investing any money in your company. My consulting group's corporate positioning statement is, "The MAS Group helps companies increase revenue, market share, and profitability through marketing alignment." Our value proposition is about targeting corporations with specific profiles and growth potential, and helping them realize that potential through our marketing alignment services.

Corporate positioning can be broad reaching or it can be pretty darn specific. It really depends on the size of the company, the markets it addresses, and the level of market leadership the company has achieved.

Two examples of more broadly defined positioning statements come from two of the largest and most successful companies in the world, IBM and GE. If you visit IBM's Web site, www.ibm.com, you will find that IBM's combined positioning and mission statement says: "At IBM, we strive to lead in the creation, development and manufacture of the industry's most advanced systems, software, networking systems, storage devices, and microelectronics." This statement is short, concise, and to the point. It tells you what they do, how they do it, and that their competitive advantage is all about leadership. What about their differentiation and value proposition? IBM's differentiation and value proposition are consolidated in the fact that they are, indeed, the leading computer company in the world and they intend to stay in that position. Leadership inspires confidence and when you buy from IBM, you can buy with confidence. Do not say your company is a leader if it is not. Too many companies are self-described leaders. It seems like the majority of the corporate statements I have read recently state that this company or that company is the leader in its respective market. You diminish your credibility if you claim leadership when you are not truly a market leader. To paraphrase Nike, just don't do it.

Does IBM mention the markets they target in positioning their company? No. It's not really necessary. They target virtually every market segment worldwide that has anything to do with information and computing technologies. When a company is as pervasive in its chosen market, it is not necessary to get specific. The same holds true for highly diversified companies. These companies compete in a number of segments of several unrelated markets, which makes it difficult, if not impossible, to tie them to a specific overall market. GE and RJR Nabisco come to mind.

Because of GE's diversification, it has to describe itself in very broad terms. A visit to the GE Web site, www.ge.com, reveals their overall positioning and mission as stated by the company: "GE is a diversified services, technology, and manufacturing company with a commitment to achieving customer success and worldwide leadership in each of its businesses. GE operates in more than 100 countries and employs 313,000 people worldwide." Companies of this magnitude do not have to be very specific in articulating exactly what products they produce and market. Nor is there a need for them to tell you that much about their positioning in any one specific market. After all, GE is a highly diversified global conglomerate and it manufactures thousands of different products that

## Chapter Five: The Marketing Alignment Remediation Process

range from light bulbs to jet engines. Its mission and/or positioning statements speak more about its worldwide leadership. Given the fact that GE's revenues in 2001 were $125.9 billion and IBM's 2001 revenues were $85.9 billion, it is not surprising that companies of this size would describe themselves in more general terms and point to their leadership positions in all of the markets in which they participate.

Apple Computer describes itself in more specific terms: "Apple is committed to bringing the best personal computer experience to students, educators, creative professionals and consumers around the world through its innovative hardware, software, and Internet offerings." Apple tells you what it does: it provides its customers personal computers, hardware, software, and Internet offerings. Apple also tells you the specific markets it is targeting: students, educators, creative professionals and consumers around the world. Its differentiation and value proposition revolves around bringing the most innovative products in the areas of personal computer hardware, software, and Internet offerings. Apple's self-description was taken from an Apple Computer press release, "Apple Presents iPod," dated October 23, 2001. Apple has an excellent understanding of its position in the market place, its target markets and customer segments, and its competitive advantage. If you want to review a company's corporate positioning statement and cannot find it easily on their Web site, just pull up one of their press releases and go to the end of that release. Companies almost always end their releases with a self-description that will serve as their CPS.

Xerox Corporation has had a rough time making the transition from the leading manufacturer of copiers to a technology solutions provider over the last few years. It would appear that some of its problems were the result of confusion about its position in the market place and its vision for the future. On its Web site, www.xerox.com, Xerox describes itself this way: "The Document Company, Xerox provides solutions to help you manage documents—paper, electronic, online. Whether you run a small business, global enterprise, or a home office, we offer high-value hardware, software services, and solutions to help you do more, faster, more easily." After reading this, it is somewhat hard to discern exactly what Xerox does, and whom specifically it is targeting with its products. Its products, services, and market targets appear to be all over the map—which is not necessarily a good thing. Company direction has to be accurately defined in order for a company's employees and its customers to understand its position in its market and its competitive advantage. You make the call.

The other extreme might be companies that are too specific in describing themselves. E.piphany is a well-known enterprise software developer with a successful track record. It specializes in Customer Relationship Management (CRM) software applications. When visiting E.piphany's Web site, www.epiphany.com, and clicking on "About Us" I was presented with this quote by Roger Seboni, its CEO: "We are leading the industry in providing intelligent customer interaction software for the customer economy incorporating a single enterprise-wide view of the customer across all touch points to cement customer loyalties and drive profitability." Do you think that farmer in Iowa would understand the message? Is this possibly a little too specific? Can we ascertain from this description exactly what the company's position, differentiation, and value proposition is within the CRM market space? Probably not. Maybe he was addressing a group of corporate Chief Information Officers that possessed a high degree of CRM experience and knowledge. Let's hope so. To be fair, delving deeper into their Web site, there is a section referred to as the Company Backgrounder which provides a better, more general description: "E.piphany (Nasdaq: EPNY) is the leading provider of intelligent software for the Customer Economy. In the six years since E.piphany was founded, it has grown rapidly and successfully, with 2001 revenues exceeding $125 million. E.piphany provides solutions for over 400 leading companies in retail, financial services, communications, technology, and travel industries, including 35% of the Fortune 100."

This is a much better and informative description of what E.piphany really does. And it tells you which markets the company targets with its CRM offerings. But why should I have to search the site to find this information? And why isn't it the first statement listed under the "About Us" section? These are navigation and content issues. If you spend any time searching the Internet for corporate positioning statements and mission statements, you will find a wide variety of documents, some of which hit the nail on the head and some which really do not tell you anything worthwhile about that company's positioning or competitive advantage. Some companies really don't get it when it comes to Web site design and content, or how it fits into the overall scheme of marketing alignment. We will discuss this more when we address the messaging element of alignment.

If your company's corporate positioning statement does not meet all of the requirements set forth in this book, then redraft it. Since corporate positioning is the essence of the company, you cannot take this lightly and throw it together in a couple of hours. Sit down with your management team and hash it out. If you need to call an offsite meeting to avoid the distractions of day-to-day operations, then by all means do that. This is probably the most important document that will be created inside your company. It is the foundation for your business model as well as your product and marketing strategies. Understand what it should contain and what it should not contain. Make sure that your staff has done adequate market research to validate your strategy and direction. A comprehensive view of the market, its predicted future direction, and its revenue and growth potential, as well as your competitors' vision and strategies will be necessary for this exercise. Get as many thoughts and ideas from your management team concerning the content of this document as you can. And you will have to insist on complete and total consensus from your management team before the document is finalized. And it would behoove you to go through this process with your management team at least once a year, every year from this point forward.

## *Corporate Positioning Statement Checklist*

Once you have completed the remediation on your corporate positioning statement, check it to ensure it addresses these items and meets the following requirements:

- Company vision and direction
- The competition
- Alignment with competition
- What the company does
- How the company does this
- Why your company is better than the rest
- Compelling company differentiation
- Why the company is better than its competitors
- The company's value proposition

- Products, services, or other offerings
- Targeted customer segments
- The company's competitive advantage
- The company's undisputable claim
- Alignment with current customer, influencer, and partner expectations
- Market leadership potential
- Clarity, coherence, and consistency
- Is this statement short and concise—will it pass the elevator test?

## *Product Positioning and Value Propositions*

The next step in the marketing alignment remediation process is to determine if your product positioning is on target or if it needs some modification. Your alignment review process should have revealed any inconsistencies or issues relating to your product positioning. It has to be in alignment with your corporate positioning as well as the requirements and expectations of your market space. Was your corporate positioning and your product positioning perfectly aligned? If not, then you and your team will have to redraft your product positioning documents. Maybe your company has entered some additional or different markets from those targeted in the previous years. Or possibly your target market has evolved radically and its requirements are so different that your original corporate positioning is no longer relevant. You could have revised your product offerings to match the new market requirements, but not your corporate positioning. If that is the case, then corporate positioning needs to be updated. Even though your direction might have been altered somewhat, your vision for the future and your company's values should not have changed. Your first job is to bring your corporate positioning and product positioning back into alignment. Examine any changes you have made to your product value proposition and how it differs from your company's value proposition. Also review any changes in the expectations and the requirements of your target market segment that will impact your product and/or corporate positioning. Then make the appropriate revisions to your corporate and product positioning to bring them in line with each other and market requirements.

Next evaluate your product positioning statement to ensure that it addresses what your product does, how it does this, how it is different, why it is better, and its value proposition. You have to address each of these items to make sure that you are communicating the right message to your potential customers, partners, and influencers. A partial message will not get the required information to these audiences. Your product's story needs to be complete. Especially important to the content of your product positioning statement is the communication of the product value proposition. It will state specifically the customer segment you are targeting with this product, the product's specific application, and its competitive advantage. The value proposition is the seed you plant to create the must-buy attitude in the mind of your intended customer. Your product value proposition must include an undisputable claim that your competitors cannot make. Ensure that your competitive advantage is still relevant and that it coincides with the most salient benefits desired by your target market segment. You will also have to ask yourself this question: Will this value proposition enable my company to achieve market leadership in the market segment that it is targeting? It should meet all of these criteria or you should consider rethinking your entire product strategy.

In the battle for market leadership in the online airline ticket sales market, an excellent example of a solid value proposition has emerged recently. In their advertisements, Hotwire.com demonstrates their competitive advantage over Priceline.com and Travelocity.com. From market research, Hotwire.com determined that the two most important factors to potential customers using such a service are: (1) getting the lowest price (2) not having to give out credit card information prior to choosing a fare. In their commercials, Hotwire.com interviews potential users of this type of service and demonstrates Hotwire's low price advantage over Travelocity for a specific destination. In this same commercial, Hotwire.com does not even bother to compare Priceline.com's price because Priceline.com requires a credit card number prior to the price search. Hotwire mentions this in their ads and explains that is why they don't even compare prices with Priceline.com. By determining what features are most important to potential customers and then demonstrating your competitive advantage in these areas, you can create that must-buy attitude in the mind of your targeted customers. And after all, isn't that what your value proposition should be about?

Your value proposition will have to coincide with the market or markets you are currently targeting. Ensure that they do. If they do not, then your value proposition will have to be revised and recreated. Make sure that your market research is up-to-date. You are using this information to validate your product and marketing strategies. It had better be current. Your company's success depends on it. Also, make sure that if you make any changes to your product value proposition, that these changes are reflected in your marketing strategy and plans. Markets are not static. In fact, remember that you are operating on Internet time. This means that things change so quickly you could miss a significant event or trend if you or one of your team members misses the daily business news. If there is too much going on in your market space for one person to keep up with, assign an appropriate number of staffers to monitor the latest market news and intelligence. In fact, the more members of your staff following your markets, the less chance there will be of missing any important events or announcements. Such events or announcements could impact your current strategies. Stay current with the latest market trends and events affecting your market space. Your company and your own success depend on it.

You surely do not want to be left in the dust by your competitors. The best way to hedge your bets in this situation is to have more and better intelligence on your market segment or segments. In reviewing your product strategy, reevaluate the resources required to effectively compete in your chosen market. Can you achieve market leadership in your current target market? If there is a question, you should revisit your value proposition and possibly revalidate it. If you are unable to make the necessary changes to your product offerings to remain competitive, maybe you should consider market segmentation. Choosing a more lucrative customer segment target could very well help you achieve market leadership.

First, study the latest research on the growth potential and life span of your current target markets. Get any data available on the individual segments of your current target market. Determine if your product value proposition would have a greater appeal to a more specific segment of your target market. Would your product be a better fit for that segment? Would you have to make any modifications to your product for it to be competitive in that segment? Be sure to compare the cost of selling in your current market to the costs of selling in other possible target seg-

Chapter Five: The Marketing Alignment Remediation Process  139

ments. Estimate the potential market share you could achieve in each market segment. Compare the projected growth and revenue estimates for your current market and the other target segments. Ascertain what factors, if any, would shorten or lengthen life of your chosen target market and your products.

Your product value proposition and positioning have to be aligned with your target market or market segment. Sometimes this is an easy call and sometimes not. According to an article in *Inc. Magazine* dated July 1, 1999, when Knight-McDowell Labs of Carmel, California launched their first product, Airborne, there were a number of market segments they could have targeted. Airborne is a natural effervescent tablet designed to provide instant immunity when venturing into germ-laden environments such as schools, hospitals, and airplane cabins. The company offered a solid value proposition and excellent differentiation. The product's claim would have been difficult to prove without extensive clinical trials. It has been legitimized by natural foods retailers. The dietary supplement market, which exceeds $14 billion in total revenue, is the overall market for such products.

Rather than take on the entire dietary supplement market, the company chose as their primary target the airline passenger segment. The company utilized direct sales channels to reach hospital and school workers, which was their secondary target segment. Knight-McDowell's sales strategy was to market their product through selected natural foods retailers, through airport gift shops, and directly through their own Web site and an 800 number. The effervescent tablet, despite the popularity of Alka-Seltzer, is a new concept to a lot of Americans. However, endorsements from celebrities such as Kevin Costner, who requested that Warner Brothers stock the tablets on their corporate jets, helped popularize the product. The product was also endorsed by the training staff of the San Francisco 49ers. In fact, the first ad for the product outside the airline trade magazines and the Internet appeared in *The Hollywood Reporter*. As the company establishes greater brand equity, they will be able to expand their distribution and market focus. At the time the article was published, Knight-McDowell Labs projected revenues of $2 million to $2.5 million for the year 2000 up from $600,000 in 1998. They were wise to limit their market targeting to specific market segments, as well as limit their distribution channels, in the early stages of the product life cycle. Over time, the company's brand equity and financial resources will expand and allow

Knight-McDowell Labs to widen both their target markets and their distribution channels.

Keep in mind that entering a smaller segment of the overall market will not preclude your company from expanding into the larger overall market once you have achieved the necessary momentum in the initial market segment. Ping started with putters and now is one of the largest golf club manufacturers in the world. Cannondale started with bicycle trailers and is now one of the largest bicycle manufacturers in the world. New Balance began making arch supports and is now one of the biggest athletic shoe companies in the world. Win the small battles first and you will put your company in the position to win the bigger marketing wars.

The other side of the market segmentation equation has to do with successful market leaders in the larger, overall markets refocusing their divisions to target specific market segments with more specialized products. A couple of examples that come to mind are Nike and Casio. Nike began life as an athletic shoe manufacturer and marketer. You know the story. Phil Knight, the student, and Bill Bowerman, the coach, meet at the University of Oregon in 1957. Knight goes on to Stanford Business School and writes a market research paper about breaking Germany's domination of the U.S. athletic shoe industry with affordable, high-tech exports from Japan. While Knight is studying business, Bowerman is handcrafting shoes for his track athletes who are breaking records right and left. In 1964, Knight and Bowerman each contribute $500 to their newly formed company BRS, Blue Ribbon Sports, and they are off and running. (Pardon the pun.) By the way, they paid student Carolyn Davidson $35 for designing their trademarked symbol, the swoosh, back in 1971. In 1980, Nike goes public. By 1982, the company has over 3,000 employees and has moved into marketing Nike apparel as well as shoes. The company goes on to create one of the most successful businesses in America, and one of the most successful branding campaigns of the twentieth century. Nike reported revenues for fiscal 2001, which ended in May of 2001, of $9.5 billion. Not bad for a company that makes sneakers.

Over the years Nike has widened its product lines and narrowed its market focus to specialized targeted segments that include: Nike Basketball, Nike Running, Nike ACG (outdoor hiking, climbing, kayaking), Nike Jumpman23 (can you say Michael Jordan?), Nike Soccer, Nike Golf, Nike Goddess, and Nike Hockey. The bottom line here is that Nike realized early on that once they established their brand equity globally,

## Chapter Five: The Marketing Alignment Remediation Process    141

they could segment their target markets and use their superstar athlete endorsements to help them gain the required momentum to dominate each market segment that they decided to enter. Nike's differentiation and competitive advantage is all about incorporating innovative, leading-edge technologies into their products and combining that technical innovation with major superstar endorsements. That is how they built their company and that is still the current strategy. Based on their performance to date, I would say they have an excellent strategy and on target to continue to be very successful.

Another example of market segmentation by a market leader is Casio. Casio was one of the first companies to manufacture and market inexpensive digital watches. The company has been a market leader in the digital watch market and has expanded its product lines quite a bit over the years. Casio introduced a premium digital watch model several years ago called the G-Shock. The watch is quite popular among the outdoor, adventure seeking weekend athletes. The watch is priced in the $70 to $100 range. It is very rugged, durable, accurate to within plus or minus 15 seconds a month, and can survive in watery depths of up to 200 meters. It also has the stopwatch, split time, and lap counter features of most sports watches. Very macho, right? For sure. It takes a licking and keeps on...well, you know where we're going with this.

Casio determined that one way to increase its market reach with sports digital watches would be to target young women who were sports-oriented as well. Who would have thought you could sell a sports type digital watch to that market? Casio did the homework and discovered that there would be some changes to the original design required, but nothing the company's product development department could not handle. So they created the Baby G. It is smaller, more compact, comes in designer colors, but it is just as rugged and even has the added telememo feature. The telememo feature will allow the user to keep 25 sets of data such as the names and telephone numbers of 25 of your closest friends. Casio has since added this feature to a couple of the larger G-Shocks. I suspect the telememo is more attractive to women and girls than men. It is available in different languages as well. In any event, the Baby G has been quite successful and has provided Casio with additional revenue streams for digital watch product lines.

Casio's differentiation and competitive advantage for the G-Shock and the Baby G is about combining cutting-edge technology with reliability, durability, accuracy, and style. Casio has done very well with this strategy in all of its targeted segments. Even leaders in larger overall category markets can expand their reach using market segmentation. Besides manufacturing watches, Casio also manufactures calculators, cash registers, clocks, musical instruments and keyboards, cameras, personal PCs, label printers, portable TVs, and a number of other products. The company reported 2001 revenues of over $3.5 billion.

Make sure that your product positioning and your product value propositions are in true alignment with your company positioning. Develop your product value propositions based on the most current market research and intelligence. Study your competitors and determine your competitive advantage. Ensure that your product's value proposition includes that undisputable product claim that your competitors cannot make, and that undisputable claim creates a must-buy attitude in the mind of your targeted customer. Choose the market segments in which your company can compete most effectively and ultimately achieve market leadership. Constantly monitor your markets and watch for trends, events, and announcements that can impact your company and product's position in your market segments. Ensure that customer, market, and influencer expectations and requirements line up with your company and product positioning. Also, be very mindful of the costs of selling into your targeted market segment. Ensure that the revenue potential available from that segment is in keeping with your revenue plan. Build the spreadsheets, run the numbers, and make sure that the return on your company's investment and profit projections are in line with your expectations. In the immortal words of Steve Martin, in his portrayal of the character Navin R. Johnson in the movie *The Jerk*, "It's a profit deal?!?" That is exactly what it is.

## *Product Positioning and Value Proposition Checklist*

Check your product positioning and value proposition to ensure it addresses these items and meets the following requirements:

- Alignment with corporate positioning
- Alignment with competition
- What the product does

## Chapter Five: The Marketing Alignment Remediation Process

- How the product does this
- The product's differentiation
- Why the product is better
- The product's value proposition
- Product application
- Targeted customer segments
- The company's competitive advantage—undisputable claim
- Market research and customer surveys validate this proposition
- Market segment dynamics—growth, revenue, and longevity
- Alignment with current customer, influencer, and partner expectations
- Resource availability to attack targeted market segment
- Channel alignment with targeted market segment
- Emerging trends or disruptive technologies that could impact market segment viability
- Clarity, coherence, and consistency
- Is the product value proposition short and concise—will it pass the elevator test?
- Market leadership potential in the targeted segment or segments

*Sales Channel Strategies*

The third step in the marketing alignment remediation process is to fix your channel strategies if they are not on target and need revision. Your sales channel strategies should be aligned with your corporate and product positioning. This means that your sales strategy should be in harmony with your company value proposition and product's value proposition. Whether your sales channel strategy utilizes your own internal sales organization, external channel partners, or both to move your products to the ultimate consumer, the approach used and the value proposition broadcast by your sales organization and/or sales channel partners have to match the overall messaging broadcast by your company. The sales organization's vision, values, and direction also have to be in alignment with those of your corporate mission. If you built your sales channel organization a few years back, you might wonder how these elements could be out of alignment. Market requirements change over time. Sales and/or channel organizations evolve over time. Your sales channel strategy should evolve with the market and other external forces, but that does not always happen.

When your company began life, things were probably much simpler than they are today. That, of course, depends on just how young or old your organization happens to be. Your company could have chosen the best, leading-edge sales channel strategy and kicked butt during the early years, but as your product's market matured, the selling requirements could have changed significantly. Earlier in the book, Lotus Development Corp. was cited as example of a company that defied convention by creating a direct corporate sales organization to target a market segment that heretofore had not been targeted by PC software vendors—corporate America. And within a few months of the introduction of their new integrated spreadsheet software, Lotus became a market leader. Prior to Lotus coming on the scene, spreadsheet vendors had sold their products through distributors to computer dealers, who primarily targeted small business customers and professional business people. Lotus determined that corporate America would embrace personal computers if they had a killer application to drive that revolution. Lotus was that application. Lotus took this concept one step farther by using a direct sales force as the mainstay of their sales and channel strategy. The Lotus product was an immediate success and corporate America did indeed embrace the PC platform as the next wave of office technology. The fact that IBM had just introduced their first PC a year earlier gave legitimacy to the whole effort. In fact, IBM's PC sales tripled in the first three months following Lotus' introduction of Lotus 1-2-3.

The Lotus story brings up two important points regarding the sales strategy paradigm. First, if you do your homework, you could buck the current trends and go with a sales strategy that defies the prevailing logic and methodologies being employed in your market space by your chosen competitors. And if you are very diligent about doing your homework (market research) and guess correctly, you could become a market leader overnight. Remember, the definition of luck is when preparation meets opportunity. Lotus understood the opportunity and was well prepared when the time was right. Bold tactics such as those taken by Lotus should only be attempted after thorough market research and strategy validation. Point number two has to do with what happens once the market begins to mature. Do you think Lotus only embraced the direct sales strategy that made them so successful? If you said yes, then you would be wrong. Lotus also employed the traditional channel strategy that utilized distributors and computer dealers/resellers. Never overlook the strategies that your competitors use, even if you have come up with a new innovative channel strategy that goes against conventional logic and practice. I dare say that in the long run, Lotus sold more software through the traditional distribution channels than it did through its direct sales force. Their direct approach gave them the notoriety and credibility needed to be successful in the other sales and distribution channels.

Now let's talk about target alignment between your company and your sales channels. It should be quite obvious that your sales channel organization, be it internal or external, should be targeting the exact same market segments that your value proposition indicated were the most appropriate segments. You will have to ensure that your sales channel partner's targeted segments have not changed over time. Review this item on a regular basis. Sometimes channel partners change direction in midstream. Maybe they believe that they've discovered a more lucrative target market segment and are now pursuing it. Possibly they hired a new marketing manager who thought he or she could generate more business by targeting a different segment. Or maybe your sales channel partners added some new product lines that appeal to a new and different audience.

Communicate frequently with your sales organization and/or channel partners. You and your team should spend some time on the front lines with the sales people. Get feedback on every aspect of your sales channel operations. Gauge customer receptivity to your offerings and programs. This will help you determine whether or not your sales team and channel partners are adhering strictly to your product's positioning and value proposition. It will also tell you whether or not your customers are still buying into your product's value proposition. It will bring to the surface any other problems that are thwarting your sales efforts. To ensure your targeting is still appropriate and accurate, have your sales team and channel partners gather as much of this information from your customers as possible during the sales process. What we are talking about here is profiling to ensure correct targeting, along with a modicum of customer satisfaction measurement. The results of these surveys will also help you determine if your channel programs are in alignment with your company and product value proposition.

If this not appropriate or possible during the sales process, have other members of your staff survey an adequate sample of your customer base on a regular basis. Getting a picture of how your customers think, act, and spend will also provide you with a reality check on your marketing and channel strategies. In most cases, you can learn more about the effectiveness of your sales strategy, your marketing programs, and your product promise from informal customer feedback than from any other source. Customer profiling will help you determine if your targeted segments and the actual segments you are reaching match up. And possibly it might cause you to rethink your current targeting strategy. If you do rethink your targeting strategy, do not overlook the issues impacting your channel strategies and how you're going to achieve alignment if you change your targeting model.

Your analysis of your sales channel strategy should have included a review of your sales team and channel partners to ensure that their approach and messaging reflected the values, vision, and direction of the company, as well as the product value proposition. If your sales team, be it internal or external, does not practice what your company preaches, your customers will be confused and may be reluctant to do business with your sales team or your company. For example, if a healthy portion of your value proposition involves customer service, and your sales team does not practice and promote customer service, then the customer will believe that your sales organization and your company are misrepresenting the offering. Translate that to mean: "We won't be doing business with you in the future." Or if your sales team cannot articulate the product's benefits and competitive advantages using the same message as your company's advertising and product literature, then the customers will believe that the company and its representatives are speaking from both sides of their mouth, which invalidates any claims or promises that are made. Again, the result is lost sales and market share. Be it their approach or messaging, solid communication systems and frequent training can successfully overcome this problem. That is, assuming you hired the right people and selected the most appropriate channel partners.

## Chapter Five: The Marketing Alignment Remediation Process

Discovering that your sales team and/or channel partners are not using an approach that is in keeping with your company's values and differentiation normally uncovers a deeper problem. The problem could be inappropriate selection or inadequate training. If the approach is lacking or radically different from expectations, you should first survey key customers doing business with this sales team member or channel partner. Identify specific problem areas, and then determine if this situation is the result of poor selection or inadequate training. Once that determination is made, you can take the appropriate action to remedy the situation. If the problem does not seem to be pervasive throughout the sales channel organization, then the problem is most likely the result of poor selection. If better communications or additional training cannot remedy the problem, then you will need to find a replacement for that person or partner.

If you discover that the problem exists throughout your sales organization and channel partner network, then it is time to perform a comprehensive review of your sales channel communication systems and your training curriculum. Somewhere down the line, there are some very serious communication problems. If your marketing and training divisions cannot properly communicate the company's market approach and value proposition to the sales channel, then you had better analyze the problem and come up with a solution quickly. Time is money. Involve everyone that has a part in sales training and corporate communications. Get as much input and feedback as possible before any restructuring or change management initiatives are implemented. A wholesale reorganization of your sales organization and channel partners can be catastrophic if not thoroughly researched and thought out. You cannot force your sales team or channel partners to implement a wholesale change in their approach with existing customers. An equally bad idea would be to take away existing customers from your sales reps, particularly if they have spent several years developing these relationships. Imagine what would happen if you committed both of these no-no's.

In 1999 Xerox implemented a sales force reorganization that almost single-handedly brought the company down. After many years of successfully selling Xerox's big, expensive copiers, Xerox salespeople were told that there was a new initiative and that they would be selling document management "solutions." Top management came up with a plan that required Xerox's sales reps to change their approach, and begin selling outsourcing contracts, software and services along with the hardware they had been selling. To compound the problem, the sales reps were reassigned from their familiar territories to focus on industry segments. Sales reps who had spent years developing relationships with key customers had to abandon them and start fresh with a number of customers with whom they had no familiarity.

Imagine what would happen to your sales organization, and your revenue streams, if you mandated that your sales team give up their best customers and present a totally new sales approach to a completely new set of customers who had no history with these sales reps or channel partners. Transitioning to a new segment of your original target market with a product customized specifically for that market is one thing. Retargeting the same customers with different members of your sales force and channel partners to sell basically the same products is suicide, particularly when your sales reps have spent years successfully developing solid relationships with these customers. It just doesn't make sense. This isn't just a bad idea; it is a horrible idea. Don't do it...wouldn't be prudent...period.

Other sales channel strategy considerations have to do with the market leadership concept. Make sure that you have enough channel partners to meet your revenue and growth objectives. Be realistic in setting your company's revenue and growth objectives. Be realistic in determining how much each of your channel partners can contribute to your revenue and growth. This isn't nuclear physics. It's Sales Management 101. You should have data from each of your partners outlining their current and projected revenue production. Then simply calculate what percentage of their revenue production your product or products will represent. Measure it each quarter, and revise your numbers based on their performance. If you need more channel partners to meet your objectives, then add additional partners. Do not add channel partners that will take away sales from your existing channel partners unless the existing ones are not performing up to expectation. Channel conflict is not a good thing...ever.

Speaking of channel conflict, there was a software vendor who will remain nameless that will serve as an excellent example of channel conflict. There was a vice president of sales who always seemed to be overly optimistic about meeting quarterly sales quotas. And he would do whatever it took to meet these objectives. This scenario involved three-tier software distribution, so I will provide you with some additional information on this distribution model. Software vendors sell to distributors, who sell to resellers, who sell to the ultimate consumers of the product. In the

## Chapter Five: The Marketing Alignment Remediation Process

past, software vendors were notorious for loading their distributors with too much product at the end of each quarter in order to meet their quarterly sales objectives. Keep in mind that most software vendors were publicly held corporations and were judged on their quarterly performance. In fact, their stock price depended on it. Normally the software vendors would promise the distributors additional marketing and advertising programs to help them move the product in the next quarter.

In some cases, the vendors would provide the distributors with very attractive financing or terms to get them to purchase that much product. Both the vendors and the distributors always knew exactly how much product the distributor could take based on that distributor's inventory at that point in time, and their weekly sales for that product. Now back to the story. One quarter, after this sales VP had convinced his distributors to take more product than they could possibly sell to their resellers in the upcoming quarter, he went directly to the resellers and offered them the same products at a cost below the cost they were paying those same distributors. Not only did he load the distributors with too much inventory, he loaded up their customers, the resellers, with these same products. And he did this by offering the resellers a better price than the distributors could offer those resellers. Sales Vice Presidents don't last long when they employ such tactics. You should always think win/win with dealing with any of your partners. If your partners don't succeed, how can you expect to succeed? You won't remain in business very long by achieving your goals at your partner's expense.

Do not over-distribute your products. This goes back to the win/win concept. If you reduce your sales channel partners' ability to sell their fair share of your products because you sign up too many channel partners, then you are doing both them and your company a disservice. You could take a "survival of the fittest" channel partner approach, but this is not really advisable. Besides being unfair to your channel partners, it could very well reduce the perceived value of your offering. It has to do with old macroeconomic supply and demand formula. An over-supply of your products could cause price devaluation, which in turn will reduce the product's perceived value. The other side of the coin is producing a slightly smaller amount of product than demand would indicate. This is a common phenomenon. Think about it. Remember when the new VW Beetles hit the showrooms? They sold for more than their sticker price. The first Mazda Miatas enjoyed the same fate. In the early nineties, Compaq and Toshiba enjoyed the same phenomena with their most popular notebook computers. Some business strategists believe over-distribution is never a problem. Others advocate the opposite approach. Just think win/win and you will develop successful and long-lasting relationships with all of your channel partners.

Equipping your sales organization with the all of the tools required to do their best job should be an integral part of your sales channel strategy. Make sure your sales team and channel partners have everything they need to do the very best selling they can. Most problems related to inconsistent sales approaches and the dissemination of misinformation have to do with the lack of proper training and/or sales collateral materials—brochures, data sheets, spec sheets, case studies, success stories, white papers, etc. With regard to training, the best measure for the effectiveness of your sales training programs is hitting your numbers—achieving your sales goals. The second measure is customer retention. If your sales team and channel partner's approach is on target, your customers will buy and keep coming back for more. If your sales numbers do not meet your projections, this is the first place to look. And with the pervasiveness of the Internet, dissemination of new information should never be a problem. This holds true for updating sales collateral materials and getting them out to the field. Your Web site should contain everything your sales team and sales channel partners require to do their job. Color printing can be expensive, but for getting new literature out to the field in a hurry, this is your best solution. Your sales team should never be able to say that their ineffectiveness has to do with the lack of current information or literature on your products.

The marketing, channel, and promotional programs that your company provides should be in line with the revenue production levels your company expects to achieve. This will be included in your annual budget projections and will be a specified percentage of your projected revenue. Make sure each component of your marketing expenditures has an anticipated return on the investment and is measured accordingly. Any marketing program that cannot demonstrate a return should not be included. There are always members of the marketing staff that will argue that some programs are not measurable or will impact revenue at some time far off in the future. Be very wary of any marketing efforts that you can't quantify. Some of these programs will be national end-user marketing campaigns to stimulate demand for your products. Other programs will provide a direct connection to your channel partners selling organizations to help each of them hit their sales quotas. Every program should be measurable.

Regardless of the types and number of programs your company provides, the messaging has to be consistent with your company and product positioning, as well as your product value proposition. Your sales channel partners should provide some level of marketing to help promote your company, your products, and themselves. Your company can help subsidize these marketing efforts through co-op funds based on your channel partner's sales contributions or through joint promotions with your channel partners. It is up to you to provide your channel partners with the appropriate marketing tools and content to achieve this end. The level of marketing support you provide to any one-channel partner will have to match their revenue producing potential. Make sure that you have someone that oversees any channel partner marketing programs or campaigns that involve your company's products to ensure that the messaging and content is in line with your own messaging, positioning, and value proposition.

Channel partner selection is a critical factor in the success of any organization. Just remember that selection criteria must include the following elements: (1) potential to help you become a market leader; (2) matching targeted customer segments; (3) unwavering belief in your value proposition; (4) similar values and adaptation of your recommended sales approach; (5) ability to offer the required levels of sales, service, and support; (6) parallel vision of the market place and its potential; (7) adequate resources to accomplish your joint objectives, and; (8) ability to provide complete geographic coverage of markets. Whether you are just starting out, or expanding your current channel organization, you should apply these selection criteria to all prospective channel partners. Do not add partners just to raise your sales numbers. In the end, they could do your company more harm than good if they are not carefully screened and meet all of your requirements. Compare their potential to their past performance. Ensure they are up to the task and have the resources to make it happen. Selecting sales channel partners is no different from hiring sales people. Be very selective and only opt for the very best. If your partners cannot help you achieve market leadership, then why bring them aboard? Your company's future depends on this. Review your sales channel strategy carefully. Then take whatever steps are necessary to bring it into alignment with your other sales and marketing elements.

## Sales Channel Strategy Checklist

Check your sales channel strategy to ensure it addresses these items and meets the following requirements:

- Alignment with corporate positioning
- Alignment with your product positioning and your value proposition
- Sales team and selected channel partners that can help your company achieve market leadership
- Sales channel strategy meets or exceeds the strategy of the market leaders
- Strategy matches your channel partners' targeted customer segments with your company's targeted customer segments
- Your sales team and channel partners employ the correct sales approach and process
- Channel partners provide an adequate amount of marketing and promotional programs to meet their sales projections
- Your company provides your sales team and channel partners with all the necessary sales tools and collateral
- Your company provides your sales team and channel partners with all of the training necessary for them to be successful in selling your company's products
- Your company provides your sales team and channel partners with the appropriate amount of sales support and service
- Your sales team and channel partners differentiate themselves in a similar fashion to your company's differentiation
- Your sales team and channel partners can help you achieve your stated revenue and growth objectives
- Your sales team and channel partners provide you with required geographic representation

- Your sales team and channel partners share your company's vision, values, and direction
- Your sales team and channel partners provide the same levels of sales, support, and service your company advocates
- Your company provides the necessary marketing, channel, and promotional programs to make your sales team and channel partners successful
- You haven't saturated any geographic areas with too many channel partners

*Messaging*

The fourth step in the marketing alignment remediation process is to examine the results of your messaging alignment review and determine which messaging elements need revision. Messaging encompasses everything written or verbalized by every employee or partner. It includes every executive or corporate presentation, every advertisement, every piece of sales and marketing collateral, every influencer communication or presentation, every investor relations presentation or communication, every product manual, every customer service script, every product package, every bit of content on your Web site—basically every word produced, printed, or broadcast by your company. It is a very big job just to keep track of all of this content. It is an even bigger job to see to it that all of this content is in alignment with your corporate positioning, your company's value proposition, your product positioning, and your product value proposition. As daunting a task as messaging alignment might seem to be, it is considerably more straightforward to review, analyze and correct than the strategic components of your sales and marketing alignment elements. That does not mean that you can review and fix it by tomorrow afternoon. It simply means that identifying messaging alignment issues is much easier than aligning your corporate and product strategies with customer, influencer, and market requirements. The down side of this task is that there are literally thousands and thousands of words to review if your company has been in business for any length of time.

## Executive Messaging and Presentations

So where do you start? Why not start at the top? Your executive team is no doubt on the road constantly—talking with investors, analysts, the press, partners, suppliers, government officials, high-visibility customers, and a myriad of other folks. They're making presentations of all types. Sometimes the presentations are corporate overviews, new product releases, or maybe new product directions. Sometimes they relate to fundraising junkets, or damage control—such as justifying positive or negative quarterly results, talking about mergers or acquisitions, or explaining significant headcount reductions. In most cases, these executives are using presentations to make their case, profile the company, or announce the latest product release. These presentations are generally created by the marketing department, and should hopefully be in alignment with the corporate and product positioning. Yes, they should, but that doesn't always happen. There are instances where the executive, whether it's the CEO or VP of Sales, dictates the content of the presentation to an administrative assistant. Hopefully, the CEO understands the relevance of aligning his presentation with corporate and product positioning, but not always. New executives are not as likely to make the connection. In some cases, new executives think they have a better grasp of the situation. This maybe hard for some of you to believe, but not only is it possible, it happens. Marketing staff members don't usually argue content with high-level executives. Too many high-level executives shoot from the hip and believe their BS to be unassailable.

Not true. Corporate consistency is imperative, regardless of how smart you think you are. Even if you're shifting your corporate direction, you have to come up with a transitional message that will mesh with the company's previous direction. Your new direction and corporate positioning should be a derivative of your previous corporate positioning and direction. How can you expect anyone to buy into a strategy or value proposition that has no connection to your company's evolving history? You can't. By the same token, every presentation given by every executive in your company should follow the company mantra—your company's positioning and direction. After all, your company was built on this positioning and this direction. Your company's value proposition is based on its positioning and direction. Its competitive advantage is based on this positioning. Remember…what do you do, how do you do it, how

## Chapter Five: The Marketing Alignment Remediation Process

is it different, why it is better, and your value proposition. These are the keys to the kingdom. Use them frequently and effectively.

Here is an example of an aligned executive presentation taken from a recent speech by Michael Dell, CEO of Dell Computer, at the Department of the Navy's *Connecting Technology Conference* in Virginia Beach, VA on May 15, 2001:

> "Due to our direct relationships with customers like the Navy, we've been able to listen and respond to what customers want, when they want it. Those insights have been our guide as we develop our range of products and services. Thanks to the relationship we're building as members of the NMCI project, Dell and EDS yesterday announced an alliance to jointly market products and expertise in the United States as a 'one-stop shopping' source of computer systems and technology services. Under our new agreement with EDS, we will sell client computer systems combined with EDS services. Dell Web hosting opportunities and desktop management service offerings will be part of the offerings."

Even though Michael was speaking about a new Navy project, Navy/Marine Corps Intranet, in which Dell was partnering with EDS, early on he emphasized Dell's primary corporate and product positioning, which has to do with direct selling relationships, rapid needs analysis, and custom computer configurations. He goes on to mention other Dell competitive advantages such as onsite customer service and quick turnaround. Michael also used the speech to emphasize Dell Computer's commitment to enterprise computing, networking, mobile computing, wireless computing, and the company's most recent focus on developing the best line of computer servers available. He covered all of the bases and continually reinforced the Dell value proposition of offering a complete line of custom configured systems, solutions, and service direct to the customer. The contents of this speech were taken from Michael Dell's personal Web site, which is a part of Dell Computer's Web site at www.Dell.com.

The CEO better know from where he or she speaks. It is imperative that the CEO promotes corporate positioning, as well as the company's value proposition and direction, in every speech, briefing, and conversation (on or off the record). The problems that emerge with regard to executive presentations and corporate alignment are more likely to occur in presentations being made by executives that are not involved in sales, marketing, PR, or product development. Financial, manufacturing, and operations executives are more likely to focus on rhetoric relating to their own areas or domains, and less likely to articulate corporate positioning and direction. Just be cognizant of the executives that are most likely to broadcast messages that are not truly aligned with your corporate and product positioning. Monitor them closely until you are confident they understand the importance of maintaining alignment. Even then, it's not a bad idea to develop a system for the purpose of reviewing the content of every executive presentation to ensure true marketing alignment.

## Advertising Messaging

When it comes to messaging alignment, advertising should be a slam-dunk. That is, unless your company's advertising creation and content is contracted out to an ad firm. Even then, your corporate marketing staff and executives should be signing off on every advertisement prior to its initial run. In fact, your product team should sign off on every step of the ad creation process rather than wait until the finished product is unveiled. This is standard procedure in established companies, but younger companies are not always savvy about such matters. Any ad agency worth its salt will require a close working relationship with its clients and make sure they are involved in the process from concept sign-off to final proofing. Generally, the early stages of concept development involve sign-off on the images, copy, and content of the proposed ad. The advertising agency's account manager and project leader should also understand the importance of marketing alignment and messaging consistency. If they don't, go find a new agency.

If there is no agency involved, then your marketing and creative group will develop the ads. Internal ad development does not preclude the requirement for an overseer or a content monitor. Sometimes the marketing and creative people get so caught up in a new approach or ad concept that they forget the product's original positioning and value proposition. Maybe they're looking for an opportunity to blindside the competition with a new slant on the competitive advantages of your product. Regardless, an objective set of eyes and ears should review the content to make

## Chapter Five: The Marketing Alignment Remediation Process 157

sure that it matches the product's current positioning and value proposition, and is still appropriately aligned. The marketing alignment coordinator can provide this objective viewpoint. There is a caveat here. If the newly appointed marketing alignment coordinator is part of the marketing organization and has to review content created by his or her superiors, just make sure that there are no job security issues associated with critical reviews of their superiors work. If need be, appoint an arbitrator to rule in such instances. That will take the pressure off the marketing alignment coordinator.

If your company is highly diversified and markets a plethora of unrelated products, there should be an overriding corporate theme embedded in each ad, as well as consistency with regard to look and feel. It is imperative that each ad not only address your corporate positioning and direction, but it will have to meet the expectations and requirements of your customers, influencers, and the overall market segment you are targeting. If your value proposition validation market research is still current and on the mark, then this should not be an issue. Given the dynamics of the market and the rapid evolution of corporate and product development, it is still a very real possibility for one or another of the elements to slide, ever so slightly, out of alignment. This is exactly why there should be a marketing alignment coordinator—some person or group to continually monitor every alignment element of your sales and marketing efforts. This must be done on an ongoing basis. Your alignment will most certainly slip during the evolution and development of your company and its products. You cannot just perform the alignment once and expect it to stick. Continuous review and monitoring means continuous review and monitoring. Do it.

Kelly-Springfield Tire Company has been in business since 1894. The overriding theme and company line is "A good deal on a great tire." Value is the primary competitive advantage espoused by the company. I noticed a two-page advertisement placed by Kelly Tires in Athlon Sports™' 2002 edition of *Golf*; an annual publication about (you guessed it) golf. You might think that an ad that takes up two full pages would include a substantial amount of copy pertaining to performance, handling, safety, durability and other practical advantages of Kelly tires. You would be wrong. They do mention handling and limited warranties, but there are only a total of four lines of text in this ad. Three lines on page one and one line on page two. The background for this advertisement is a photo taken from the front of a long traffic jam. The camera puts you right in the middle of two lanes of traffic looking back about twenty cars. The photograph provides the total backdrop for the ad and takes up both pages. The left page reads as follows:

> This is a traffic jam.
>
> It's the same traffic jam you sit in, whether you bought expensive tires or not.
>
> But the guy with the Kelly tires gets to sit on a bigger wallet.

The copy on the second page reads:

> With long-mileage limited warranties and great handling, Kelly is all the tire you need.

Can you see the alignment between the company's positioning and this ad? It is as clear and concise as the ad itself. Not a lot of wasted words here. It relates the value proposition as clearly as it can be related. Nothing fancy, but it is effective. It would certainly pass the Iowa farmer test in communication viability. Kelly sees part of their targeted market segment as those guys that would rather spend their money on golf equipment instead of tires. We know that a portion of the golfing community is made up of the country club set. That would probably not be the target market segment for this company. However, a larger segment of the golfing population (about 80%) is made up of duffers and hackers that hang out at local municipal courses. This segment would definitely be more value conscious. Kelly has a good handle on who comprises their market. And Kelly's advertisement is very well aligned with its positioning.

Speaking of targeted customer segments, a major consideration with regard to messaging has to do with aligning your messaging with your targeted customer, influencer, and market expectations, not to mention the requirements of said constituencies. Your market research should have uncovered exactly what your customers expect, exactly what the influencers in your market space expect, and any other expectations emanating from within your market space. Meeting these expectations is absolutely critical in the development and creation of your messaging. Once you

## Chapter Five: The Marketing Alignment Remediation Process 159

have validated your competitive advantage and determined that it creates the necessary must-buy attitude in the mind of your targeted customers, it is essential that you effectively communicate that advantage in your messaging. Not just somewhere in your ads or product presentations, but as the prevailing theme in those ads and presentations. If your advantage is truly an undisputable claim that represents the expectations of your customers, make sure it doesn't get lost in the message. Remember the Kelly Tire Company ad. It doesn't take a lot of verbiage to get your point across.

Another ad campaign that comes to mind in pushing its brand, its competitive advantage, and matching its target market's expectations is the Taco Bell campaign. The company's "Think outside the bun!" campaign takes the company's strategy head-on against its primary competitors—the fast food burger emporiums. Whether they are pushing burritos or their latest "Border Bowls," the company knows exactly how to differentiate itself, meet its target market's expectations, and get its message across. I am sure that these guys have done a hundred man-years of market research to determine that fast food customers would like options and alternatives to the same old burger and fries routine. Is it too simple, too complicated, or a no-brainer? You decide, but it's been quite effective for the company.

In the June 2002 issue of *Business 2.0* online, there was an article titled "New Rules for Battling Goliath" or "How to go head-to-head with Microsoft—and Win." Rule number three was "Innovate or die." Whether you are in technology or tacos, it truly applies. Behemoths like Microsoft might produce terrible first versions of their products, but you can be sure that they will keep coming at you with new and improved versions or models until they get it right and beat you. Give them an inch and they will take a mile. If you just rest on your laurels without advocating and implementing a continuous improvement strategy yourself, your company will lose and die. Just remember to align your continuous improvement campaign with your customer's desires and expectations. You can bet that the "Goliaths" will be matching their product development with the customer's expectations and requirements. You have to be there first and maintain the lead. And your messaging has to convey your positioning, competitive advantages, and your value proposition. See to it that these elements are not buried in the copy of your ads, promotions, or programs.

Your messaging has to align with the expectations and requirements of your target customers, the influencers, and other market forces.

Speaking of influencers, why should you consider the opinions of the influencers in developing your value proposition and messaging? How could a bunch of journalists, editors, analysts, and thought leaders know more about the desires and the needs of your customers than you do? Or than the customers themselves? If the influencers' opinion becomes a primary consideration in the customer's decision process, then you have to use that information in developing your value proposition and messaging. If the influencers do not play a role in the customers' decision process, then their opinion is inconsequential. If your customers buy into their arguments regardless of plausibility, then you will have to use that to your advantage. Your competitors certainly will. Market research will tell you what influences your customers' buying decisions. Understand these influences and incorporate them into your positioning and value propositions. Then make sure your messaging reflects these realities. Influencers' sway depends on the product category. Companies producing inexpensive consumer products are not usually affected by influencers in the same way as the producers of more expensive or more technically-oriented products. In most cases, the influencers play no role in the decision process of customers who purchase lower-priced consumer products. This is why it is so important to understand how your customers make their buying decisions and what factors influence these decisions. You should be able to uncover this information from your customer surveys during your market research phase. Leverage this information to ensure that your product value proposition and your messaging accurately reflect the driving forces impacting your customers' buying decisions.

## Your PR Group and Messaging

Your PR department broadcasts copious amounts of content in their press announcements and press releases. In most small to medium-sized companies, the PR group is part of the marketing department. In larger corporations it is either a separate entity or part of the individual product groups. Regardless of organizational structure, the PR group has to be monitored the same as any other corporate department to ensure that the content of every announcement and release aligns with corporate positioning, product positioning, and product value propositions. You might think, "Hey, these guys know the corporate and product lines better than anyone else." Hopefully, they will know and articulate the company line better than anyone else, but don't blindly accept this premise. Do not leave them out of the alignment monitoring process. You can't afford to allow misaligned, off-message press releases or announcements to be broadcast nationally or globally. If you do, then you're compounding your marketing alignment problems. There have to be checks and balances in PR and marketing. I am not advocating the creation of a bureaucratic monitoring organization that prevents the timely release of corporate and marketing messaging. Your marketing alignment coordinator can ensure that your press releases and announcements are aligned with your corporate positioning, product positioning, and product value proposition. If they are off message or off target, then rewrite them so that they are on message and on target. The best remediation is to catch these mistakes on the front-end rather than having to implement a damage control strategy. Just remember that you cannot fix these releases after they have been released. Once a press release goes out—it's gone.

Press releases normally have two parts. The first part is the announcement. That will be the section requiring the most scrutiny. The second part is a brief corporate overview—the "About XYZ Corporation" section. The corporate overview is normally the corporate positioning statement. You remember the definition—what your company does, how it does this, how it is different, why it is better, and the value proposition. Generally this part is the same in every press release or announcement. The first part, the announcement, is the section that will require review. We're not talking extensive rewrites, but simply a quick review and alignment check. If there are any issues, it shouldn't require major revision, but rather a little wordsmithing to get it back into alignment. Here is an example of a press release that meets all the requirements of true alignment:

### INTRODUCING MACH3™ COOL BLUE FROM GILLETTE

> **Boston, January 8, 2001** -- The Gillette Company today introduced MACH3™ Cool Blue, a new razor that combines the advanced shaving technology of MACH3™ with an eye-catching, icy blue-colored handle and organizer. The new razor's color, which capitalizes on recent design

trends, was selected for its global appeal, particularly among young men.

"Our research has shown again and again that color — when combined with superior performance — can play an important role in a man's choice of razor," said Elena Fernandez-Bollo, Vice President, Grooming Products, The Gillette Company. "With blue as the current color of choice for cutting edge products from skiwear to personal computers and wristwatches, our choice for a re-colored MACH3™ became an easy one."

MACH3™ provides men with the closest shave in fewer strokes with less irritation, while the ergonomic handle provides a secure grip. The handle — now available in "Cool Blue" — features three rubberized crescent-shaped grips and is easy to hold and maneuver throughout the entire range of shaving motions.

The introduction of MACH3™ Cool Blue follows the Company's highly successful introduction of MACH3™ in 1998, sales of which have reached $1 billion. Today, Gillette holds more than two-thirds the dollar share of the global razor market.

MACH3™ Cool Blue will be supported by a print and broadcast advertising campaign with the tagline, "Move to the Cool Blue World of MACH3." The razor will be available in North America and Europe beginning in February 2001, in food, drug, convenience, and mass merchandise stores. The suggested retail price in the U.S. is $6.49 - $6.99, including razor, organizer and two cartridges.

Headquartered in Boston, Mass., The Gillette Company is the world leader in male grooming, a category that includes blades, razors, and shaving preparations. Gillette also holds the number one position worldwide in selected female grooming products, such as wet shaving products and hair depilation devices. In addition, the Company is the world leader in alkaline batteries, toothbrushes and oral care appliances.

## Chapter Five: The Marketing Alignment Remediation Process  163

This is a simple straightforward press release. If you read Gillette's corporate positioning statement—the last paragraph in this press release—you will notice that their corporate positioning is all about being the world leader in male grooming products, as well as their other product lines—female grooming products, alkaline batteries, toothbrushes, and oral care appliances. This positioning message is reinforced in the body of the press announcement in the section where the company mentions that the MACH3™ has reached a billion dollars in sales. The release goes on to point out that the company holds more than two-thirds of the dollar share of the global razor market. This is what alignment is about—tying your product positioning to your corporate positioning. And you could have learned something extra here, if you didn't realize the significance of color in branding and marketing personal grooming products. You probably did not realize that the icy blue color has global appeal.

There is one other thing about this announcement that is relevant. That is, that this announcement is obviously not targeting customers, since Gillette provides information on their advertising campaign and schedule. This announcement is directed towards analysts and the press. Consumer product companies generally do not target customers with their press releases and product release announcements. The influencers are the targets. The consumers are targeted with the companies' marketing messages when announcing new products. These messages are broadcast through the media, both print and television, and through point-of-sale advertising and promotions.

If your company has an analyst relations group or a PR group that takes on the AR responsibility, the remediation process will also address any issues uncovered during the review process concerning your company's analyst relations presentations and messaging. If there are analysts involved in helping your customers determine what product to purchase, then it is very important to revise all messages originating from your AR group that don't meet alignment standards. If analysts have a direct influence on your customers' buying decisions, then you had better make sure that your messages targeting them are in true alignment, and that you have taken their feedback and input, and incorporated it into your product's positioning and value propositions. Remediation is about addressing the issues and fixing the problems. Review, analyze, and compare…then fix any messaging problems that have been uncovered.

## Your Sales Team and Messaging

The group that will probably need the most scrutiny with regard to messaging is your sales group. Yes, it is the producer of revenue and responsible for fueling the engine that drives your company into the future. The sales group's role is critical to the success of any company. It just happens to have direct access to your customers and frequently produces its own marketing collateral materials without necessarily understanding the importance of sales and marketing alignment.

I have been a marketing director, a product manager, and a sales director responsible for seventy-five million dollars in revenue annually, not to mention Managing Director of the European Division of a network software company with full P&L responsibilities. My position has always been that if you have a viable product in a viable market, your marketing department's job is to make your sales group's job easy. Don't get me wrong; both groups are integral to the success of the organization. Unfortunately, they don't always work in concert with each other. So let's address that issue.

Your first objective should be to enlighten your sales team and sales channel partners about the importance of sales and marketing alignment. Their objective and primary goal is to move product. They will generally use whatever means necessary to accomplish that goal whether it meets the criteria for successful sales and marketing alignment. This is not an indictment of salespeople, sales groups, or sales divisions, or their management. It is just what they do if they are not included in or made aware of the strategic importance of maintaining sales and marketing alignment. Their jobs and their revenue production capability will be improved significantly if they maintain alignment. There are a number of opportunities for the misalignment to occur. This is particularly true if direct lines of communication between sales and marketing are not in place.

For example, your company introduces a new product or a new version of an existing product, and the sales reps out in the field have not received the new data sheets and/or product brochures. Their first impulse will be to create their own marketing collateral materials. And in doing so, they could use a value proposition that is not in alignment with the company's value proposition or that of the overall product line. They might emphasize a feature that happens to be the feature du jour for that market...one that every product on the market includes, and one that will not properly differentiate your product. Or possibly they could emphasize

## Chapter Five: The Marketing Alignment Remediation Process  165

price in their collateral when over half of your competition offers more aggressive pricing. Chances are that the marketing thrust of the sales-created collateral will not be that far off the mark, but if marketing is broadcasting one message and sales is broadcasting another message, there will be a very real possibility that these inconsistent messages will create market confusion and damage the salability of your product or products.

This situation can be easily corrected. With the emergence of the Internet, there is no excuse for sales groups not to have access to the most recent, up-to-date marketing and collateral materials. The marketing group can create these materials and make them available on-line to all of your sales reps anywhere in the world. These materials will include data sheets, product brochures, product line brochures, price lists, volume discount schedules, upgrade information, product recall information, user guides, case studies, success stories, and the latest print advertisements, as well as product and corporate announcements. About the only thing that the sales group might need to create themselves would be proposals, if those were germane to the sales process for your products. Even then, the marketing alignment coordinator should review the proposal template and make sure it is in true alignment with corporate and product positioning.

Another area where sales reps can sometimes miscommunicate corporate or product positioning is in verbal communications. If your sales reps interact directly with your customers or distribution partners, it is imperative that their sales pitches be reviewed, analyzed, and approved by your marketing group or the marketing alignment coordinator. It is probably more likely for a sales person to misspeak the company line or the product's value proposition if they interact with the customers or distribution partners extemporaneously. Most salespersons have a gift for gab, but if their pitch is not in keeping with the company and product's positioning, then another opportunity for inconsistent messaging rears its ugly head.

Whether your sales people work with your customers or distribution partners face-to-face or over the phone, it is absolutely essential that their messages be coherent, compelling, and consistent with your marketing alignment. Creating scripts for your telesales folks or in-person pitches for your outbound sales reps should be a joint effort between sales and marketing. Don't be surprised if your sales management is not keen on this idea. Most sales managers and sales executives feel no one is better equipped to write or create the pitch than the sales team themselves. You can allow this if the marketing coordinator or marketing team has an opportunity to review these messages prior to their implementation and ensure they meet the alignment criteria. If sales and marketing can work on this together, the final product will most likely be a better, more cohesive message, but if that does not seem feasible, then let the sales team craft the message and have marketing review it.

Setting up regular meetings between sales and marketing will help eliminate confusion about messaging and create more synergy between the groups. The meetings do not have to be onsite or face-to-face if your sales team is scattered out across the country or across the globe. You can do it via telephone conference, the Internet, or videoconference. The main thing is that the meetings are held on a regular basis, such as once a month or once every two months. The meeting should be structured and have an agenda, and it should also include a forum with enough time set aside for discussing issues, problems, solutions, opportunities, and success stories. As I said before, marketing's primary objective is to make the sales person's job easy. The only way marketing will be able to accomplish this objective is to understand exactly what goes on during the sales process. If there is no dialogue between sales and marketing, then this will not happen unless your marketing team is telepathic. If your company uses third-party sales reps or sales channel partners, invite them to participate in the S&M meeting, or at least set up separate meetings for them with the marketing team on a regular basis as well.

If your company does use third-party sales reps, distribution partners, or other sales channel partners to sell your products, the chance for inconsistent messaging increases substantially. There are several ways to keep these folks in the loop and on message. Regular meetings between your company's sales and marketing teams is the most important ingredient. Regular training of these partners is the first step in helping them stay on message. Providing them with easy access to sales collateral materials, product updates, press releases, and other pertinent company and product information via the Internet will also contribute to their success. Regular visits from company sales and marketing team members will ensure that your sales channel partner's needs are being met and provide your company with the necessary feedback. It will allow your sales and marketing team members to witness their approach and messaging in person on their turf. There is no better method of determining what's going on out in the field and in the trenches with the customers than being there to see it first-hand. E-mails and telephone conversations are important, but will not provide you with the true reality of witnessing the sales process from their viewpoint.

Once all alignment issues regarding your sales team and sales partners have been identified, it is up to you to see to it that they are prioritized and assigned to the appropriate person for remediation. These are not issues that you can sit on. Your revenue is the lifeblood of the company, and anything that adversely affects or impacts your revenue stream should be prioritized to the highest level. If you cannot instill the proper sense of urgency in those persons involved in the remediation process, you should replace yourself.

## Your Training Group and Messaging

If your sales and product training is carried out by a group or department not affiliated with your sales or marketing departments, then that group will have to be brought up to speed on the alignment issues, and then monitored on an ongoing basis. In some instances, the training group doesn't realize or understand the importance of staying on message. They are generally more concerned with sales approach and methodology than content. If they are involved in product training, they could very well be focusing on product specifications, capacities, or capabilities as opposed to positioning and competitive advantages. In either case, this team will need to be advised and indoctrinated on the importance of sales and marketing alignment, and its relationship to the sales process and the communication of the product's features, attributes, and benefits.

The common practice for most companies is to utilize product managers, product developers, or engineers to train the sales team and other company employees on the intricacies and capabilities of the product. Sales training is typically carried out by sales managers or directors. If it is at all feasible, it is be best to combine product and sales training. By combining the two, you have a better chance of integrating company and product positioning into the sales process and the accompanying messaging. With some product types, this is just not feasible, but you can still combine the most appropriate approach, presentation, and messaging in the sales training. If your company engages third-party sales reps or channel partners, your training program for these partners will determine whether or not your company achieves success or failure in reaching and selling into your targeted market segment. Train the trainers and involve them in the alignment process; otherwise, your company will have no chance in succeeding in your chosen market.

The bottom line here is to provide all of the members of your sales group, company sales team members, and third party partners with the resources, support, and knowledge to get the job done. Make sure they completely understand and buy into the marketing alignment paradigm. If you don't do this, don't expect them to stay on message and in alignment with company and product positioning or value propositions. In addition, you will have to make sure that your sales team and sales partners meet the expectations and requirements of your customers, influencers, and the overall market. And this applies to your customer support team as well. Bring your sales and support teams into the marketing alignment process, and you will be taking a big step towards ensuring that they understand their mission and their marching orders. They will be more likely to carry out their mission successfully if they can see the big picture. Remember that these guys are not mind readers, so if you don't supply them with the information, tools, and appropriate messaging, you shouldn't expect them to be able to maintain alignment in their sales presentations or other interactions with your customers.

## Your Web Site and Messaging

The final messaging conduit for your company is your Web site. If you and your team have done your homework, then every message that your company prints or broadcasts is also available on your Web site. Content on your Web site should include all of your marketing collateral, your current advertising collateral, your product's specifications, capacities, and capabilities, your case studies and customer success stories, your corporate background information and history, your corporate mission and positioning statements, any of your company's executive presentations that are pertinent, your sales collateral, your customer and technical support information and response capabilities, your sales channel/other strategic partner's information and links, your corporate and product press releases, announcements, and contact information, upcoming corporate events and announcements, dealer and retail outlet locations and information, etc.

## Chapter Five: The Marketing Alignment Remediation Process    169

Virtually everything about your company and its products should be available on your Web site. This content should be available both in Web format as well as an easily printable format. All of this content falls into one of the marketing alignment categories and should be revised as often as its printed counterparts. As your content changes and evolves, be sure that your company's Web site reflects these changes. A stale Web site will not encourage visitors to return.

Of course, if you've brought all of your sales and marketing components into alignment then the content on your Web site will be in alignment. That is, assuming your company updates your Web site frequently and checks the accuracy and timeliness of your Web site's content. If you sell your products direct, your Web site may represent an additional sales channel for your products. That would make the alignment accuracy of your site even more critical (if that were possible). The key factors in building an exceptional Web site are: (1) ease of navigation to and from each area; (2) completeness with regard to corporate, product, service, sales, and support content; (3) daily or weekly updates to keep it as current as company resources allow; (4) ease of transacting business; (5) ease of accessing/downloading sales and marketing information; (6) failsafe security for all transactions, regardless of whether they are with customers, suppliers, or other partners, and; (7) all content meets sales and marketing alignment criteria. Your Web site is your company's window to the world. If it does not comply with all seven success factors, then you had better fix it immediately so that it does comply. Never underestimate the impact of your Web site on the success of your company.

## Messaging and Remediation

Remediation requires recrafting all messaging and content that is not compelling, consistent, and in alignment with your company and product positioning, and your product's value proposition. Maintain a constant vigil on market events and trends, so that your alignment addresses the expectations and requirements of your customers, the market influencers, and the overall market. Monitoring your alignment with regard to messaging and ongoing remediation should be written in stone. It is critical in maintaining market momentum, achieving your revenue goals and market share growth, and keeping marketing costs in check.

## Messaging Alignment Checklist

Check your messaging to ensure that it addresses each and everyone of these items, and meets the following requirements:

- Your CEO, VP of Marketing, or corporate communications manager has communicated and continues to communicate the value of messaging alignment to all corporate divisions, departments, and employees
- There is a marketing alignment coordinator, messaging coordinator, or messaging coordination team to monitor all corporate and product messaging
- All messaging is in alignment with corporate positioning
- All messaging is in alignment with your product positioning and your product's value proposition
- All advertising content meets sales and marketing alignment criteria
- All messaging is in true alignment with customer, influencer, and market requirements and expectations
- Company and product press releases and announcements are in true sales and marketing alignment
- Properly align all presentations and messaging that target analysts who influence your customers, your market, or the press
- Ensure influencer input has been considered and appropriately incorporated into all of your messaging
- The sales team's approach, collateral materials, presentations, and proposals are in true alignment with corporate and product positioning and product value propositions
- The approach, collateral materials, presentations, and proposals of third party sales reps, distribution partners, and/or sales channel partners are in true alignment with corporate and product positioning and product value propositions
- Corporate Web site's content meets all alignment criteria
- Corporate Web site utilizes a design appropriate for your company's stature and position in the market

## Chapter Five: The Marketing Alignment Remediation Process

- Corporate Web site is attractive and easy to navigate
- Any and all transactions on your Web site are totally secure
- Access to sensitive data in the customer and supplier sections on your Web site is secure
- All corporate, product, and sales training content is in true alignment with corporate and product positioning and product value propositions
- Your organization currently has a mechanism in place to review all corporate messaging and content—from executive presentations to advertising, sales and marketing collateral, press releases, training materials, partner messaging and collateral materials, investor relations communications, Web site content, influencer presentations, etc.

### *Targeting*

#### Customer Segment Targeting

Just to refresh your memory, in this text the terms *market segment* and *customer segment* are interchangeable. Markets are made up of customers. As you will remember from Chapter Two, targeting is not just about markets, market segments, or customer types. Companies have to include partners and influencers when fixing their targets in the battle for mind share and market share. Alignment must involve everything a company does in preparation for the marketing wars. If an organization intends to run like a well-oiled machine, alignment should impact every aspect of the organization. Targeting is an integral part of this alignment process. Traditional marketing types believe that targeting is only about markets and customers.

Marketing Alignment requires not only aligning marketing efforts with market and customer segment targets, but also achieving alignment with both market influencers and channel marketing partners. *Influencer targeting* involves identifying those outside parties that exert the most influence on your targeted customer's buying decision. It is up to you to see to it that their views and feedback are incorporated in the marketing alignment equation. Influencers include journalists, editors, analysts, and thought leaders in your chosen market segment. *Partner targeting* is about identifying and developing strategic alliances with the most appropriate sales channel and total solution partners. Your marketing alignment review should have revealed the appropriateness or inappropriateness of your current customer, influencer, and strategic partners. Now the remediation can begin.

We will begin with customer targeting. In performing the market research for your value proposition validation, you determined the specific customer segment that would be most compelled to buy into your product's value proposition. If your market research was correct, then your product's undisputable claim created a must-buy attitude in a significant percentage of the population of this market segment. Having said that, you might wonder "How on earth could my customer segment targeting require any remediation?" Possibly your marketing programs are not reaching this segment or they are not hitting the bull's-eye. Maybe they are reaching the overall market audience, but not the more specific market segment target. If that is the case, you will have to do some additional surveys to determine the exact demographic profile of the segment you're reaching and compare that profile to the profile of the segment you need to reach. Once you have determined that you are not reaching the desired segment, you will have to figure out how you can reach that market segment. Remediation in this context is all about devising a plan to reach the most desirable customer segments consistently.

It is possible that your sales and distribution channels are on target, but your advertising vehicles are not reaching your segment. In other words, your sales channels are the most appropriate sales venue for this segment, but your advertising or promotions or both are not drawing this customer segment into your channel's sales outlets. You might have the right products in the right place, but your ads are bringing in another segment. Or possibly your advertisements are reaching a broader audience than you had envisioned when you chose the publications in which to place your ads. In either case, you will need to rethink your advertising or promotions strategy and do the required market research to identify the most appropriate publications or media vehicles.

It is conceivable that you provided your market research findings to your advertising agency and they chose publications or other media that they believed would reach your targeted segment. If you have discovered that your advertising is not spot-on target and effective in driving the most

## Chapter Five: The Marketing Alignment Remediation Process 173

appropriate customers into your sales channel outlets, then your will have to reevaluate the publications or other media you or your ad agency selected. If you and/or your marketing team chose the media, you re-evaluate and revise your media choices. The advertising salespersons should have provided you with detailed demographic profiles of their readership or viewership.

If your sales team or sales channel partners believe that your advertising is not reaching the right customers, then you should call the magazine and/or other media ad sales reps to the carpet and determine why your advertising is not producing the right results. You shouldn't have to commission a survey of the readership of each of these publications to ascertain the demographic profiles. Examine every media vehicle where you have been advertising and determine if their audience profiles exactly match the demographic profiles you identified during the value proposition validation. You cannot always rely on what their salespeople tell you, so get a sample list of their subscribers and do the surveys in-house. In reality, this is something you shouldn't have to do yourself, but if that's what it takes to reach your target market segment, then do it. In fact, it wouldn't hurt to survey small samples of the viewers and readers of your chosen advertising vehicles to validate the accuracy of the their stated demographics, if you have the resources to do this. If not, then demand to see current validated demographic information or drop them.

There is another possibility. Your advertising content could be appealing to the wrong segment of the advertising vehicle's audience. This is a messaging problem. You will have to go back and compare the message in your ads to your original value proposition and get it back in alignment. If you think it's too late, you're wrong. The sooner you straighten it out, the sooner your plan will be back on track. Better to fix it now and achieve proper alignment than throw away any more advertising dollars. It is more likely that you are reaching the wrong audience than broadcasting the wrong appeal, but it won't hurt to go back and check it out. Considering the relationships between your value proposition and your targeted market segment, you might need to revisit your value proposition and revalidate it. You should have done this in the initial stages of your marketing alignment review, but the market dynamics are such that markets can evolve and change in a matter of weeks. Targeting should be fixed during value proposition validation, but if it's not working then go back and revisit the strategic elements of your marketing alignment construct.

Targeting can be easy and straightforward when done correctly. While looking through the May 2002 issue of *Motor Trend* magazine, I noticed a two-page advertising spread for the Honda Civic *Si*. Given the fact that the magazine targets car enthusiasts, I was somewhat surprised that Honda would advertise the Civic. Performance doesn't necessarily come to mind when you think of a Honda Civic and Honda produces several other V-6 powered models better known for their performance. The Civic *Si* model, however, comes with a 160HP motor, which is a lot of power for a sub-compact car. The ad shows three cars sitting in a parking lot with their doors lying on the pavement while the Honda Civic *Si* is driving away. The message, of course, is that this little econobox has just blown the doors off the other cars in the parking lot. Honda is targeting budget-minded, performance oriented car enthusiasts with this particular Civic model and that correlates with the readership demographics of *Motor Trend*. The value proposition for this particular product is low initial price, economy, reliability, quality, and performance. The ad imagery and content fits perfectly with the target audience. Honda does an excellent job in matching the Civic *Si*'s value proposition with its target audience. Honda cemented the deal by selecting an advertising vehicle whose readership matched the demographic profile of the Civic *Si*'s target audience. This is how targeting is supposed to work.

The primary considerations with regard to targeting are: (1) make sure that your targeted market segment correlates exactly with your product's value proposition; (2) use market research and customer surveys to validate that your product's undisputable claim/competitive advantage creates a must-buy attitude in the mind of your targeted customer segment; (3) ensure that the market segment your company is targeting will provide the best return on your marketing expenditures; (4) verify that there is not another market segment that your company could target that would provide better revenue streams and more growth opportunities; and (5) make sure that the market segment your company is currently targeting is the most appropriate market segment to propel your company into a market leadership position.

## Chapter Five: The Marketing Alignment Remediation Process 175

### *Customer Targeting Checklist*

Check your customer targeting to ensure it addresses these items and meets the following requirements:

- Targeted customer segments match your company's and product's positioning
- Target customer segment or segments are in perfect alignment with your product's value proposition and have been recently validated
- Company sales and distribution channels target identical customer segment or segments
- Product or products your company is selling into this target market are optimized specifically for this targeted customer segment
- Your targeted customer segment or segments will provide the very best return on your marketing investments
- Targeted customer segment or segments will allow your company to expand its reach over time and put your company in a position to become a market leader
- Targeted customer segment or segments will allow your company to compete effectively with the market leaders also targeting this segment
- The cost of selling into this customer segment will not be prohibitive and reduce your profit margins to unacceptable levels

### *Partner Targeting*

Partner targeting primarily involves choosing the best, most qualified channel partners and/or total product solution partners. Selecting business partners is very much like selecting your employees. Every partner that you choose should be both strategic to your success and in alignment with your goals, values, and direction. Poor selection leads to a waste of your precious resources. Even if your company has vast resources, mistakes are not a viable option—period. If your company uses venture capitalists, or has other investors or shareholders, you can be sure they will not look kindly on poor decisions by management or wasted resources. You should have been very selective and discriminating in choosing your partners. The employee analogy is closer to the truth than you might think. Your partners are an extension of your organization. They play an integral part in your success or failure. Poor partner choices could lead to a soiled image and reputation. Conversely, being very selective and smart in your choices will produce high quality partners that will enhance your image and reputation.

## Sales Channel Partner Targeting

We will begin our discussion of partner remediation with your sales channel partners. It is not uncommon for sales channel partners to rethink their business model, their strategies, and/or their direction. If any of your sales channel partners are not living up to your expectations, it might be because they have changed since you partnered up with them. When you chose your channel partners, you selected them based on the profile of the customers they were targeting, the product lines they sold, and their similarities to your own organization in the areas of sales, service, and support. Channel partner prerequisites included strong marketing programs that paralleled your own. You chose channel partners that met your geographic coverage requirements and could produce a projected revenue stream that would help your company achieve its revenue and growth goals. Finally, you selected channel partners you believed could help your company achieve market leadership.

The marketing alignment process requires ongoing scrutiny of your partners to ensure that they're holding up their end of the bargain. Are they still targeting the customer segment you identified in your product's value proposition? Does their sales approach reflect your company's values, mission, and direction? Are they offering sales, service, and support programs that are in alignment with your company's own programs? Are they providing the geographic coverage required in your original agreement with them? Are they fairly and professionally representing your company and your company's products? Are they using the same value proposition and competitive advantage to sell and market your products? Are your partners putting the appropriate emphasis on your products compared to their other offerings, and meeting your expectations in that area? Are your channel partners living up to your expectations with regard to their marketing and advertising efforts on behalf of your company and

## Chapter Five: The Marketing Alignment Remediation Process

products? Have your channel partners been completely open and receptive to your training initiatives? Are the communications between your company and your partners open, frequent, and productive? Is the level of customer satisfaction with any of your channel partners below expectations? Finally, is every one of your channel partners meeting their stated or written revenue objectives? If any of your channel partners are not meeting all of these requirements, your marketing alignment review should have uncovered it. Least we forget; a partnership should always be a win/win situation.

Remediation of any of these issues will require that you and your partner get together and address the issues to determine if they can be quickly and easily resolved. If they cannot, then it is time to dissolve the partnership and find a new partner. Achieving true alignment requires that your partners meet all of your company's requirements. If your partner has changed his or her strategy and decided to target a different customer segment, then that is not an issue that can be resolved. That is, unless your partner is willing to create a new offering by combining your product with one or more complementary products that would be a more appropriate solution for the newly targeted customer segment. It is possible that this partner might be capable of helping your company expand its market reach into this new segment. It could mean additional revenue and more share of the overall market. It would certainly be worth further consideration and maybe some additional market research. This is the only scenario where such a situation might be beneficial to your company. If your channel partner has simply changed his strategy or business model, then it's time to initiate the search for a new channel partner in that geographic region.

There are probably as many sales approaches as there are sales channel partners. If any of your channel partners are using unacceptable sales approaches, you will need to sit down with them and understand where they are coming from and why they are using a specific sales approach. Try to understand the basis for their particular sales approach and how it will affect your company's reputation and image. Take the time to find out how it might impact the sales of your products. If the sales channel partner is using unethical or unscrupulous tactics to close sales, then it should be a no-brainer. Get rid of them. If they are simply using a technique that is specific to their particular region of the country and meeting their sales quotas, then at least take the time to understand the approach.

Make sure that there aren't any negative ramifications resulting from this approach. If there are none, and the customers seem to understand and embrace the approach and feel they are being treated fairly, it should not pose a problem. Different geographic regions sometimes require somewhat different tactics.

The main consideration regarding the utilization of different sales approaches should be ethical and fair treatment of the customers with acceptable levels of support and service. If your partners can meet those requirements and achieve their sales targets, then there really isn't a problem. If the problem is the lack of proper sales or product training, the ball is in your court and you will need to address and resolve this issue as quickly as you can.

If your sales channel partner is not offering appropriate levels of service or support, you will have to get together with that partner and determine why the level of service or support has dropped. It could be that this partner simply paid lip service to the service and support requirements and never intended to meet those requirements. If that is the case, start looking for a new partner ASAP. If your channel partner has temporarily lost part of their support staff and fully intends to get the service and support back up to the required level, then give them some time to resolve the problem. Any help you can provide will be very much appreciated, and will most likely be paid back in increased emphasis on future service and support, not to mention increased sales.

If the problem has to do with a lack of technical or product training, then you can definitely address the problem and get it fixed quickly. See to it that your channel manager has mandated that all channel partners provide training requests whenever they lose staff members or hire new staff members. If it isn't financially feasible to send someone out to train these folks on request, set up a computer-based training program via your Web site to serve as an interim training mechanism. Regional training sessions and/or training at your corporate headquarters should be scheduled at least quarterly or bi-annually.

If geographic reach is a problem, you simply need to go out and recruit additional sales channel partners in the regions that are not being adequately served. You should have handled this problem during channel development, but there could be a number of reasons why it did not happen. Maybe your company did not have the resources to service channel partners in every region. Or possibly you signed channel partners for

## Chapter Five: The Marketing Alignment Remediation Process 179

these regions and they were not up to the challenge. Regardless of the reason, if you have the resources to serve them, you should be out recruiting new partners right now. It is costing your company lost sales opportunities.

If you have channel partners that are not living up to their revenue production promises, you need to find out why. First, you will need to determine the cause of their revenue shortfall. Are they doing adequate marketing? Are they properly articulating your product's value proposition and competitive advantages in their marketing and advertising campaigns? Are they employing the proper sales approach? Have they received adequate sales and product training? Is the partner located in a region suffering from an economic downturn that is localized and not affecting other regions of the country? Are they targeting the most appropriate customer segment? Get to the bottom of the problem and get it resolved. The more time you spend helping your partners, the more time they will devote to familiarizing themselves with and selling your products. Salespeople typically do the best job selling products they feel comfortable selling. This reinforces the importance of proper training. If your sales partners are not very technical, but your product is, you would be well advised to structure your training so that only the most salient features are emphasized—your primary competitive advantages. Then provide those partners with reference materials that are easy to use and provide the most important, frequently requested information. Take the time to understand the types of tools and training that will best benefit your sales channel partners. See to it that they get exactly what they need on a timely basis.

Another issue that might negatively affect your channel partner's sales could be not providing them with adequate marketing support. Marketing support involves providing your channel partners with things like advertising artwork, logos, local ad copy and layouts, not to mention advertising co-op funds. Co-op funds represent a small percentage of your channel partner's previous quarter's sales that you rebate back to the partners. Your partners can apply these funds towards various marketing activities that you oversee. The more they sell, the more co-op they receive. Co-op generally represents 2-4% of their product purchases in the previous quarter. You should provide as much marketing support as possible to all of your sales channel partners. It is in your company's best interest for your channel partners to succeed in their respective markets.

Besides providing marketing support, it is incumbent on your company to provide your channel partners with adequate supplies of product literature and sales collateral materials. Make it available via your Web site to all of your partners. There are software applications that you can use to bolster your partner relationships. These applications will help you distribute the latest product information, press write-ups, and other pertinent sales collateral materials to your partners. The software will also provide tools for co-op fund management, order processing and tracking, and inventory control. Depending on the size of your organization, such applications might be helpful in better managing these partnerships. Providing marketing and sales support will help your channel partners do a better job with your products, and ensure that their messaging is in perfect alignment with your company and product positioning.

If your current partners are doing a good job and there are no remediation issues, you might want to look at other types of sales channel or distribution partners that could help you expand your market reach. Targeting additional market segments could very well require an additional set of channel partners. Depending on your future growth plans and ability to appeal to additional market segments, it is certainly something to consider. Determine the relative costs of venturing into new market segments and the expected gains in revenue and market share. Analyze the life cycles for each of the market segments under consideration, and the expected life span of the distribution or sales channels needed to support these segments before making any decisions. In the recent past, sales channel longevity does not appear to be that much longer in years than the product categories themselves. Remember, a long-term plan these days should encompass about two years. Sales channel partner targeting is critical to your success. Do your homework. Weigh the relative costs of entering and supporting each channel prior to entry, then determine how much revenue and growth you will gain from moving into these channels. If they meet your requirements and can help you achieve your overall business objectives, then add them to your strategic plan and begin building the relationships.

# Chapter Five: The Marketing Alignment Remediation Process

## *Sales Partner Targeting Checklist*

Check your sales channel partner targeting and programs to ensure that they address these items and meets the following requirements:

- Sales channel partners are aligned with your company's sales channel strategy
- Sales channel partners' positioning matches your company's and product's positioning
- Sales channel partners' value propositions align with your product's value proposition
- Sales and distribution channel partners target the same customer segments identified and validated in your product's value proposition
- Sales channel partners endorse and broadcast your product's value proposition
- Sales channel partners provide you with the geographic coverage and reach outlined in your sales channel strategy
- Sales channel partners' sales approach is in keeping with your company's values, vision, and direction
- Sales channel partners offer service and support programs in keeping with that of your company's recommended service and support programs
- Sales channel partners keep recommended quantities of sales collateral materials, brochures, data sheets, and other product literature on hand
- Sales channel partners are receptive to all of your company's training programs and have received all of the appropriate training classes
- Sales channel partners' messaging and marketing programs align with your company's own messaging and marketing programs
- Sales channel partners have all of the sales and marketing tools to do an effective job of marketing your product or products

- Sales channel partners participate willingly in all of the communication initiatives set forth by your company
- Your company's staff and your sales channel partners have on an ongoing dialogue concerning strengths, weaknesses, issues, opportunities, and success stories
- Each of your sales channel partners meets their mutually agreed to revenue and market share goals
- Targeted sales channel partners provide your company's products access to all the most appropriate markets

## Total Product Solution Partner Targeting

The first question that comes to mind in discussing the value of total product solution partners has to do with whether or not your company needs them. Targeting total product solution partners is mandatory if your product does not represent the total solution by itself. For example, if your company sells cellular phones, your product will be useless without a cellular service provider such as AT&T, Sprint, Voicestream, Cingular, etc. This is not to say that you could not sell them separately through electronics or department stores. You could. To those people who already have a cellular service provider. But for those folks who don't already subscribe to a service, a cell phone would be useless. The phone might be attractive and nifty to look at, but it would be better if you could actually call someone with it, now wouldn't it? And you would be considerably more successful if your company partnered up with one or more service companies because you could offer the total solution. Plus, your company's marketing efforts would be multiplied by the number of partners you had in your alliance. Total solution partners are generally complementary product vendors, and in some cases, service or support organizations depending on the complexity of the total solution. If your product represents the total solution, then you don't need partners to help you complete the solution and you can skip this section.

If your product or products require total solution partners, then you will need to determine the types and number of partners you will need to be competitive in your market. Once you have identified the products and/or services required to offer a total solution, you should court and secure partnerships with all of the requisite partners. Any remediation

## Chapter Five: The Marketing Alignment Remediation Process

associated with your total solution partner programs will involve reviewing the prerequisites for each type of partner. These prerequisites should be the same for each partner type in the alliance.

The first step will be to ensure that the total solution model includes all of the necessary elements to complete the solution. If your company manufactures snow skis and that is the only product in your arsenal, your company needs to identify and partner up with binding manufacturers, ski boot manufacturers, and ski pole manufacturers. After all, it would be extremely difficult to go skiing with only a set of skis and no bindings, boots, or poles. I suppose you could duct tape the skis to your cross trainers, but I don't believe the performance and handling would be up to par. In fact, I would be surprised if you made it twenty feet before all hell broke loose. You get the idea. First things first. You should identify all of the required elements for the total solution involving your company's product and then select your total solution partners based on those requirements. If remediation is required with regard to your total solution partners, then it is because something was missed in the selection process or one of your partners is not living up to expectations.

Similar to the changes that might have transformed your sales channel partners, your total solution partners could have evolved or simply changed strategies making them less than appropriate now. Maybe they have decided to rethink their value proposition and have chosen a new target market segment. Or maybe they have reengineered their sales channel strategy and have come up with a new distribution scheme. In either one of these scenarios, your total solution partner is not longer in alignment with you and is no longer appropriate as a partner. This simply means that you have to start the selection process again and find a new partner.

It is possible that your company and product have reached a higher level in the market pecking order than one or more of your total solution partners and that partner no longer matches your sales or marketing initiatives with regard to funding or staff resources. You will have to use the appropriate criteria for selecting a new partner or partners. Your goal is market leadership, and if any of your total solution partners have fallen by the wayside during the climb, you will have to identify and ally with partners who have similar goals and resources. Find and secure partners that meet your alignment criteria.

Of course, it is possible that just the reverse has happened and your total solution partners have outdistanced you in their climb towards market domination. You may not be an appropriate partner for them anymore and you should recognize this situation. Recruit new partners who match up more closely with your current market position and resource capabilities. Alignment is about matching your company up with other companies who have similar strategies and similar resources to fulfill strategic goals. Total product solution partnering is all about synergy. It is hard to achieve synergy with partners that do not match up in capabilities, strategies, tactics, and resources. This might sound like a step backwards, but in reality it might just be the ticket to a leadership position. Trying to partner with companies who are considerably different than your own will, in most instances, create a win/lose scenario. Guess who the loser will be. If you guessed your company, then you have cracked the code. Alignment is about commonality in purpose, resources, and goals. You know, sometimes you're the windshield and sometimes you're the bug. Aligning with a goliath will guarantee that you will be the bug.

Your primary objective is to ensure that you have constructed a total solution matrix; you have identified all of the necessary partner types; and you have recruited the best, most appropriate, and properly aligned partners to provide the total solution. There must be synergy. Your joint marketing efforts will multiply your chances of success, assuming you and your partners are in true alignment and harmony. The final goal for your total solution partner group is to achieve some mutually agreed upon level of market leadership based on the resources currently available. That is step one. Step two is to move to the next level in your march towards overall market leadership based on the increased resources you will have available once you have achieved the first goal.

## *Total Solution Partner Targeting Checklist*

Check your total solution partner targeting and programs to ensure that they address these items and meets the following requirements:

- Total solution partners have similar values, direction, and vision for the future
- Total solution partners' positioning must match your company's and product's positioning

- Total solution partners' value proposition are in alignment with that of your company and products
- Total solution partners are aligned with your company's sales channel strategy
- Total solution partners' marketing strategy matches your company's marketing strategy
- Total solution partners are receptive to bundling, co-branding, and joint marketing activities
- Total solution partners are similar in size and resources to your own company
- Total solution partners are capable of increasing your exposure, your revenue, and your market share
- Total solution partners act as partners and do not try to dictate programs, messaging, positioning, or strategies
- Total solution partners are capable of helping your company achieve market leadership in mutually agreed upon stages

## Influencer Targeting

Most businesses do not give serious or thoughtful consideration to targeting market influencers when developing their overall business and marketing plans. Influencers include journalists, analysts, and thought leaders who cover specific markets. Given the impact these individuals can have on your customer's buying decisions and your company's ultimate success, your company should target these influencers and work at building relationships with them. It is possible that because of the nature or type of products your company markets, you have determined that the influencers have little or no impact on your customers' buying decisions. If you produce and market consumer products, then that is probably true. On the other hand, if your company manufactures expensive or highly technical products, then the influencers most likely do influence your customer's buying decisions and can contribute to your company's overall success or failure. If these types of influencers have no impact on your customer's buying decision, you can skip this section. Otherwise, keep reading.

In general, most companies' executives are aware of the influencers in their market space and do what they can to court them. Although companies do include PR (press relations) groups as part of their marketing efforts, the majority does not have analyst relations managers or teams. And even those companies with PR departments have not necessarily taken the time to determine who are the most influential members of the press or analyst communities with respect to their chosen market segments. Since your company has only a limited amount of resources to devote to developing relationships with journalists, editors, analysts, and thought leaders, doesn't it make sense to identify the most influential of these groups and target only those with the most clout?

In developing a remediation plan for relationship building with the influencer community, the first thing your PR and/or AR groups should do is to prioritize the individuals in each influencer category according to market focus, exposure, and influence. If your staff does not feel competent to do this, there are some very good consulting firms that can help them get this task accomplished. You cannot build relationships with every journalist, editor, analyst, and thought leader. It is resource and time prohibitive. Besides, wouldn't you rather devote maximum effort to targeting only the most influential in your market space? If these guys are dictating buy recommendations to your customers, you'd better get that process going if you have any plans to gain market leadership. Most companies take a shotgun approach and devote equal time to every influencer, which doesn't make sense.

Once you've done your prioritization, it's time to focus on the top 10 or 15 most important and influential influencers. The number you choose to target will depend on your budget and company's available resources. Developing relationships with journalists, editors, analysts, and thought leaders requires a very specific approach. Don't try to be their best friend. They will see through that charade in a New York minute. If you approach them correctly, you can develop a friendly relationship with them over time. That is really not your primary goal here, though. Your primary goal is to understand how they view your market and discover what factors that they feel are the most important in evaluating products in your market.

The influencers can and should become an important component of your market-intelligence-gathering mechanism. Since they judge products based on what they think is important, it would behoove you to make sure

## Chapter Five: The Marketing Alignment Remediation Process    187

your products conform to their expectations and that you emphasize those advantages in your messaging. There are a number of executives who believed they knew more about what the market desired than the influencers. In some cases, that was probably a correct assumption. However, the influencers were telling the customers which products to buy based on their view of what was hot and what was not. So whom do you think won out in the long run? If you said the wily corporate executives, you would be way off the mark. The majority of wins in such confrontations always go to the influencers. If you fight them, you will lose every time. You had better find a way to work with these influencers and get them on your side. In some industries and markets, they can make your life quite miserable if you are unable to develop solid relationships with them.

Working with influencers means frequent and concise communications. Never try to use a marketing presentation or pitch when providing product information to these guys and gals. They will laugh you out of their office or right off the phone if you give them that type of pitch. They simply want to know about functionality and capabilities. A product manager who can speak objectively about the product is your best bet. They also want to speak to your customers to get real world feedback about exactly how your product provides a viable solution to their particular problem. Case studies and success stories are very acceptable to the influencers. Marketing or sales collateral is not. The influencers are not interested in fluff, only in facts and factual evidence. It is quite important that any influencer presentation or communication remains in alignment with your company and product positioning and value propositions. Just stick to the facts and be objective in providing them any and all information that is germane to their needs.

The influencers are very time-constrained, so do not waste their time or you will find yourself on their blacklists. Do not ramble on about your company or your products. Ask very direct and specific questions if you are fishing for information. If you are providing information on your company and/or products, limit that information to only those areas you believe the journalist or analyst needs to know. It doesn't hurt to ask the influencer on the front-end of the conversation what specific information you could provide that would be most beneficial to them.

Influencers, particularly analysts and editors, are egocentric. It doesn't hurt to stroke their egos by asking for their advice about product issues, product development initiatives your company is considering, and market dynamics and futures, as well as an overall view of the marketscape. Do not ask them leading questions about your competitors. If they want to volunteer competitive information, they will do so. If you don't understand why they believe some features or more important than others in products such as yours, then ask them why they value those features over others. The more time you devote to trying to understand their motivations and preferences, the better equipped you will be to deal with them and win the battle for market share. Plus, you will make them feel as if you really respect their opinions and insights. That will go along way in building a solid relationship.

Your channel partners are sometimes considered as influencers in your market space. If your customers look to your sales channel partners for advice on what to buy in a particular product category, then they are definitely influencers. It is just as important to get them on your side as the other types of influencers. The fact that you and they are already business partners gives you and your company a head start in this regard. Don't try to abuse your relationship with them by bullying or trying to buy their trust. Keep your relationship on solid ground by emphasizing win/win and offering to support them in any way that will help them become more successful. Leverage your sales channel partnerships by involving them in your communications and product discussions with the other influencers from the press and analyst communities.

Your total solution partners can also be extremely valuable assets in dealing with the press and analyst communities. The journalists and analysts that you are working with are most likely the same ones your total solution partners are targeting. Pool your resources and use your synergy to build these relationships together. If you double team the influencers and utilize the correct approach, you will gain ground much more quickly. Even with such leverage, you should not expect to get these influencers in your back pocket. That would not be prudent and would probably blow up in your face. Keep all of these relationships strictly business.

One final caveat. Do not expect to gain positive reviews or favorable recommendations from analysts in whose firms you invest a lot of money in the form of subscriptions and services. The only thing you can buy through such expenditures is easier access to the analysts themselves. The same holds true with the press and their respective publications. Just because your company spends many thousands or even hundreds of thousands of dollars in advertising with these publications does not translate

Chapter Five: The Marketing Alignment Remediation Process    189

into glowing and positive reviews for your company and its products. It will generally give you more and better access to the editors and journalists…and that's it. Use your common sense and good judgment. Be ethical in your dealings with these people and they will give you a fair shake.

*Influencer Targeting Checklist*

Check your influencer targeting and programs to ensure that they address these items and meet the following requirements:

- There is a company program set up specifically to deal with all types of influencers
- The influencers in your market space have been identified and prioritized based on market focus, exposure, and influence
- Your PR and AR departments have a plan and budget for working with and building relationships with the top 5, 10, 15, or 20 targeted influencers based on available finances and resources
- Your PR and AR managers have attended seminars or classes on how to interact with and build relationships with the influencer communities
- Market influencer communications and presentations are in alignment with your company and product positioning, as well as your product value propositions and overall messaging
- Your corporate PR, AR, and marketing groups leverage their relationships with your targeted influencers to gain as much competitive intelligence as they can without jeopardizing your relationship with any and all of these persons
- You or your staff has devised metrics for measuring the success of your press and analyst relations programs
- Your staff has determined if any of your sales channel partners are influencers and are working to leverage and build stronger relationships with those identified as market influencers
- Your staff has ascertained if any of your total solution partners are influencers and are working to leverage and build stronger relationships with them

- You have identified those total solution partners who have relationships with the same market influencers as you and are working together with those partners to enhance the relationships

*Review, Analyze, and Compare—Again and Again*

Your remediation efforts are not a one-time exercise. You will need to monitor and review your alignment frequently and take whatever actions are necessary to maintain continuous sales and marketing alignment. Markets are very dynamic and adjustments will be an ongoing effort on the part of your marketing alignment team. Your company cannot achieve maximum revenue generation and market share growth if your sales and marketing efforts aren't truly aligned. In addition, you cannot expect to optimize the return on your marketing investments. And remember that if any element in the alignment group changes, you will have to reexamine each of the other elements to make sure that they are still aligned. Maintain your alignment and your company can achieve the market leadership that you have envisioned.

# CHAPTER SIX

## CORPORATE LEADERSHIP AND MARKETING ALIGNMENT

### *Bringing It All Together*

Corporate leadership is about establishing the vision, the direction, the strategy, and the goals for your organization. These things are important to your company's success, but they alone are not enough. If your divisions, departments, and teams are not aligned and working in harmony with one another, your company will not have a chance at achieving market leadership. Sales and marketing alignment is imperative if you want to get all of your company's sales and product divisions and departments working in harmony. Marketing alignment is essential if you plan to become a market leader. Market leadership is about growing your company's revenue and its market share each and every quarter. Your profitability will depend on achieving this growth while minimizing your marketing expenses. Growth and profitability are the keys to success. For your corporate leadership to be effective, you will have to make sure that your company's sales and marketing efforts are perfectly aligned and remain aligned.

If you have no intention of accepting anything less than quarter-to-quarter and year-to-year growth and profitability, then you had better begin rallying your troops around the marketing alignment paradigm. All of your teams will have to work in concert with each other and match the expectations and requirements of your targeted market segments in order to achieve your company's stated objectives. Marketing alignment can facilitate this type of departmental synergy and market harmony. It will help you maintain the lowest possible sales, general, and administrative costs if you maintain your company's alignment.

By now you should understand exactly what sales and marketing alignment is about. Your management team will have to be educated about the elements, analysis, remediation, and maintenance of marketing alignment. You and your team's first step will be to implement the marketing alignment review process. Begin the process by selecting a marketing alignment coordinator and recruiting a marketing alignment team. If you don't have the internal resources to accomplish that task, you will have to go outside your company to identify and secure the services of a qualified consulting team to manage your marketing alignment review, remediation, and monitoring. Regardless of which route you choose, each member of your executive team and your marketing team will have to be made aware of their role in the process. Once that is accomplished, the marketing alignment review process can begin.

The team will begin by reviewing the strategic elements of marketing alignment. The marketing alignment review will always be a top-down exercise. Corporate positioning and the company's value proposition are the first elements put under the microscope. Clarity and proper positioning are the most important considerations. And never forget that your company positioning and value proposition have to coincide with the positioning and the value propositions of your products. Your vision and future direction should be incorporated into your company's strategic positioning as well. Your corporate positioning statement is the foundation for all of your company's positioning and messaging. It is also the foundation for all product positioning and messaging. Never lose sight of why they call it an elevator statement. If you cannot condense your corporate positioning statement into an elevator statement, you need to go back to the drawing board. Do some thoughtful soul searching with your management team, and come away with a CPS that conforms to the elevator statement format.

Then you can move on to the strategic elements surrounding your product or products—product positioning and product value propositions. Remember that you don't really position your products, the market does. If you do a really good job of researching the market—reading your potential customers, the market influencers, and your proposed competitors—you should be capable of creating a product positioning statement

## Chapter Six: Corporate Leadership and Marketing Alignment 193

that mirrors closely the market's perception of your product offerings. Do understand that your product strategy will have to align with your corporate strategy. Your product's positioning statement will have to reflect what the product does, how it does this, how it is different, why it is better than your competition, and its value proposition.

The product's value proposition addresses the product's specific application and the identified customer segment that will benefit most from owning and using the product. Your competitive advantage will come from the undisputable claim that you can make about your product, and it must be a claim that none of your competitors can make. That competitive advantage has to be able to create a must-buy attitude in the minds of your targeted customers. The must-buy attitude has to be strong enough to remove your competitor's products from your target customers' consideration. And don't forget that you must have the financial resources to successfully compete in the market segment you choose to target. This might require that your company target a narrower segment of the overall market in the beginning in order to be competitive. And by all means, make sure that the market/customer segment you target is the most lucrative one in which your company can compete based on your competition and product's superiority.

Once you have completed the review and remediation of the first two strategic elements you can move on to the third strategic element—your sales channel strategy. The market you choose to target and your competitor's sales channel strategy will have a significant influence on the sales channel strategy you choose. In most cases, your sales channel strategy will have to coincide with how your competitors distribute and sell their products. There are exceptions to the rule. The Lotus example outlined previously demonstrates that you can take a different sales approach using a different channel strategy and still be eminently successful...but that is not the norm. Regardless of which channel strategy you select, be sure to verify it with a large amount of compelling market research that will support your decision. Identify and select your channel partners just the same as you would screen, interview, and select key management personnel. They will be instrumental in your success. Think win/win during the selection process. Look for partners that share the same goals and objectives, and ones that match your company in strength, direction, and vision. Make sure that you have the geographic coverage you need and the revenue producing potential you need to achieve market leadership.

Never underestimate the importance of intra-company communications. Simply by facilitating bi-directional communications within departments and divisions, you can put your company in a position to always be one step ahead of your competition. Most companies have abysmal communications between departments and divisions. There is a wealth of valuable information within your company that needs to be shared. Encourage and teach active listening to each and every member of your staff. Communications are only good if people get their message across. Remember what Steven Covey wrote in the *Seven Habits of Highly Successful People*: "Seek first to understand, then to be understood." See to it that your company's internal communications systems are operating at full power and you will help your company succeed and grow much more quickly than those companies with poor internal communication systems. At this point in time, knowledge is the most valuable asset in your company. Ensure that your employees understand this and share their knowledge with each other.

The strategic segments of your alignment process will impact your messaging and your targeting. Your corporate and product positioning will determine who you will be competing against, what markets and customers you will be targeting, which market influencers you will be targeting, and which partners you will be targeting. Even though the targeting elements have not yet been addressed, the corporate and product strategies you choose will have a direct correlation to the customers, influencers, and competitors you will be targeting. Just as your sales channel strategies are the result of your positioning and target customer segment selection, your messaging will be a direct result of your corporate and product positioning and value propositions. Every component of marketing alignment is directly related to every other component, which is why alignment is so very critical to your company's overall success.

Messaging typically represents a good portion of your misalignment problems. This is especially true when there are several departments or divisions creating various company and product messages. If there is no one to ensure continuity and consistency of style, image, and content, then you're asking for trouble. Trouble in this instance translates into misalignment. Misalignment translates into lost revenue and market share. It also means wasted marketing efforts and dollars. There are so many opportunities for inconsistent messaging to occur that it should be easy to

## Chapter Six: Corporate Leadership and Marketing Alignment   195

comprehend the value of having a person or team to monitor and correct these inconsistencies.

Messaging sources include advertising, sales and marketing literature and collateral materials, executive presentations, sales presentations and proposals, investor relations materials and presentations, financial reports, customer service and support documents and mailings, influencer communications, presentations and materials, case studies and success stories, product manuals, product packages, every bit of content on your Web site—basically every word produced, printed, or broadcast by your company. You should be able to see that consistency and continuity is not going to happen by itself. That is why you will have to have a marketing alignment coordinator or team to monitor all of your company's content to ensure that it meets the alignment criteria. It is just as important to see to it that the marketing alignment coordinator or team doesn't become a bottleneck and bring your corporate content machine to a grinding halt. The system should be set up so that the revisions are performed by the creators of the content. The marketing alignment coordinator's primary role will be to monitor and identify problems, not to personally rewrite all of the company content. You can see how tedious this would become if it were structured any other way.

Messaging consistency will minimize market confusion. Market confusion, more times than not, is the primary symptom of messaging inconsistency. When one department in your company is sending the customer one message, and another department is sending a different message, you can see how it can confuse the audience. In most cases, the audience is either your customer or parties who influence your customer. Your corporate and product value propositions dictate what the message should be. Your job is to make sure that the message being dictated by your corporate and product value propositions is the same message being broadcast, communicated, or conveyed through your advertising, product literature, sales pitches, Web site, executive presentations, etc. Inconsistent messages are like strikes to a batter. Consistent messages are like base hits. If you expect to win the game and reach a market leadership position, then you had better get as many base hits as you can. Marketing alignment will help you get there.

Targeting is simply following your strategies to their logical conclusions. Targeting customers is about matching the customers you intend to reach using your marketing programs with those identified in your product value proposition validation. First, you identified the most likely customer segments in developing your value proposition. Then you initiated and completed the necessary customer surveys and market research to validate your value proposition and identify your most appropriate customer targets. Customer targeting is more about making sure that the customer segments you are targeting exactly match those segments you identified when validating your product's value proposition. You will have to carry out sample surveys on a continuing basis to ensure that the customers you are reaching are the same ones you initially targeted.

Similarly, you will have to verify that the sales channels you have chosen match those you identified when developing your sales channel strategies. You will also have to maintain a constant vigil to make sure that your sales channel partners are targeting the same customer segments that you are targeting. You will have to make sure your channel partners are employing a sales approach that is in keeping with your strategy as well as your corporate values and direction. Monitor your sales channel partners and see to it that they have adequate product and sales training, and that they are accurately portraying your product's unique differentiation and competitive advantage. Sales channel partners can change direction and/or market focus pretty quickly. It is up to you and your channel team to see to it that you have a full complement of channel partners and that those partners are all contributing their part to your overall success in the market.

If your product does not represent a total solution, you will have selected total solution partners to help you offer a complete solution for your targeted customers. These partners should complement your efforts in sales, marketing, and product value. Choosing the right partners is another critical ingredient in the alignment recipe. Be sure to select partners that can help you achieve market leadership. Do not select partners that will use you to achieve their goals without helping you achieve your own goals. It is always best to choose partners who share similar values and vision. You are more likely to attain synergy with partners who more closely match your company. Synergy is critical in a total solution scenario, and the best way to achieve that synergy is to ally with partners who reflect the same values, vision, and direction. And those who have similar resources are also more likely to help you reach the leadership position you are striving to achieve.

## Chapter Six: Corporate Leadership and Marketing Alignment

Influencer targeting is important if market influencers impact the decision-making process of your targeted customers. If your product lines are unaffected by market influencers, you will not need to address this element of the alignment paradigm. On the other hand, if you do need the endorsement of influencers, then the best thing you can do is to first cull down your targeted influencer group to a manageable level. Analyze the resources you have available for targeting and courting the influencers and determine the number you can afford to go after. Prioritize the influencers based on market focus, exposure, and influence, then work on developing relationships with this limited group of influencers, and do it right. Remember, you should never try to market your product to the influencers. Give them only the information they request and need. This is generally product features and specs, case studies, and competitive information. Use them to get as much competitive intelligence and market intelligence as you can without being a nuisance. Remember how valuable their time is and treat them with respect. Ask their advice on product development initiatives and plans, as well as market events and trends. Approach the influencers in the appropriate manner and they will give you more time than the other guys. Don't expect to attain credibility with them in the early stages of the relationship development process. Show them respect and give them what they want, and your relationship will develop more quickly. If they exert serious amounts of influence on your customers, bite your lip, treat them with civility regardless of their behavior, and it will pay off in the end.

Once the sales and marketing alignment review is complete, it's time to assign priorities to the areas requiring revision. Priorities should be assigned based on whether the areas requiring revision are strategic or tactical. Always address the strategic areas first, especially during the remediation phase. Make the appropriate changes and revisions, and you will begin to see the fruits of you efforts. Can you just leave it at that and expect everything to go smoothly from that point forward? Not really. Remember, this is the Internet Age. Everything happens at warp speed. Markets are not static, but very dynamic indeed. It is up to you to lead your company forward and adjust to the constantly changing economic and market climates. You and your company will have to innovate continually to win in the marketing wars. Innovation should touch every element of the organization on a frequent basis. The market leaders know this and will use it to beat you if you don't practice continuous innovation yourself.

Ensure that you have a person or team in place to keep your sales and marketing efforts aligned. That means continual and ongoing review and adjustments. Set up an ongoing schedule. Always start with the strategic elements first. Then move on to the more tactical pieces of the puzzle. Everything has to fit together. You do want to grow your revenue and market share, don't you? And reduce your marketing expenses as a percentage of revenue? Absolutely. That's your primary reason for being...that is, being a leader in your company. Marketing alignment will help you achieve these goals and keep your company on track to continue meeting your goals. Keep it up and your company just might be the next market leader. Who knows, you might even be the next Bill Gates. And while you are at it, begin thinking about corporate alignment. That will be the subject of my next book.

# ABOUT THE AUTHOR

An Austin, Texas native, Mac McKinley has over 35 years of business, sales, and marketing experience. Over his career, he has held numerous positions in product management, marketing management, sales management, and general management. While serving as Director of North American Sales at Artisoft, Inc., the company was named the "Number One Hot Growth Company in America" by *BusinessWeek* magazine. Mac also led Artisoft's European efforts against overwhelming odds (in the form of a newly introduced free Microsoft product), and managed to gain a market share in the face of that competition. He is a published writer, analyst, and strategist. Mac is a graduate of the University of Texas Business School. He enjoys golf, tennis, hiking, mountain biking, and sailing his catamaran. Mac established The MAS Group in early 2002 in response to the changing needs of American business brought on by recent economic trends and major market shifts. Mac believes that any company that intends to succeed in the coming years will have to implement a sales and marketing alignment program. Mac can be contacted at goalpath@att.net.

www.ingramcontent.com/pod-product-compliance
Lightning Source LLC
Chambersburg PA
CBHW030933180526
45163CB00002B/549